Multiracial Identity

Also by Mark Christian

BLACK ORGANISATION AND IDENTITY IN LIVERPOOL: A Local, National and Global Perspective (*editor with William Ackah*)

Multiracial Identity

An International Perspective

Mark Christian
Honorary Fellow
Department of Sociology, Social Policy and Social Work
University of Liverpool
and
Visiting Fellow
Institute of Commonwealth Studies
University of London

Foreword by

Diedre L. Badejo
Chair
Department of Pan-African Studies
Kent State University

Consultant Editor: Jo Campling

First published in Great Britain 2000 by
MACMILLAN PRESS LTD
Houndmills, Basingstoke, Hampshire RG21 6XS and London
Companies and representatives throughout the world

A catalogue record for this book is available from the British Library.

ISBN 0–333–71664–7

First published in the United States of America 2000 by
ST. MARTIN'S PRESS, LLC,
Scholarly and Reference Division,
175 Fifth Avenue, New York, N.Y. 10010

ISBN 0–312–23219–5

Library of Congress Cataloging-in-Publication Data
Christian, Mark, 1961–
Multiracial identity : an international perspective / Mark Christian.
    p.   cm.
Includes bibliographical references and index.
ISBN 0–312–23219–5 (cloth)
1. Racially mixed people. 2. Identity (Psychology) I. Title.

HT1523 .C48   2000
305.804 — dc21
                                                          00–020121

This book is printed on paper suitable for recycling and made from fully managed and sustained forest sources.

10   9   8   7   6   5   4   3   2   1
09   08   07   06   05   04   03   02   01   00

Printed and bound in Great Britain by
Antony Rowe Ltd, Chippenham, Wiltshire

For
Louis, Cabral, and Shelley –
who unerringly represent the millions of scattered seeds in
the African Diaspora

Contents

List of Tables

Foreword

Diedre L. Badejo

A paradox within a conundrum

Within the context of understanding peoples of mixed African and European heritage international communities, Dr Christian's book brings forth a very painful and bitter human experience that is the eldest offspring of racism, racist ideology, and the institutionalisation of racial hierarchies: that is, colourism *within* the community of people of colour. What else would one call the child of Cleopatra and Mark Antony, or the Cape Verdeans, or the Cape Coloureds, or Frederick Douglass, or Malcolm X's beloved mother, or Bob Marley, or Chaka Khan? Yet all of these socially constructed 'multiracial people' are part of the engagement of the African world with Europe, the Americas, and other parts of the globe. The articulation of the existence of 'multiracial peoples' as a special category of the human species, however, is the conundrum of a racialised European-centred world history. The paradox of such a world history is the self-denial of its own contributions to the creation of either the category or the people to whom it refers, and the false sense of superiority/inferiority that it engenders. Certainly, the purpose of this apparent paradox with this racialised conundrum is the control of the many by the few, a situation that has not fundamentally altered in more than 500 years.

Indeed, the problematising of 'mixed heritage' or multiracial children is a phenomenon of contemporary racial politics, since African women in Africa and in the African diaspora had little opportunity to ponder the woes of their multiracial children outside the confines of enslavement, colonialism, class and caste in which they were most often born. Nor did they have their own voices with which to speak or the ears of others who would listen to their lamentations and concerns about their children who were sold, bred, beaten, abused, raped, tortured and stigmatised just like their darker kin. Indeed, in our racialised psyches, there is the myth that lighter skinned blacks have or had it better than darker skinned blacks.

Yet I am reminded of a man in my childhood community who was in a southern military barracks in the 1940s when a 'race riot' broke out. His mother was a close friend to my own grandmother who sought to comfort her. Apparently, the son was summarily beaten by the whites for being a light skin black, and by the blacks for being a light skin black. In his rage, he retaliated accordingly and spent several days in solitary confinement with untreated wounds before my grandmother's friend could get him proper medical attention. He never recovered from this ordeal fully, and he spent the rest of his life in and out of mental institutions. For whites he represented their own hypocrisy, and for blacks he represented their own contradictions. To his mother he was her middle child born of a man whom she loved dearly, and whose family hated her own brown skin passionately. His unfortunate treatment is the tragic consequence of the racialisation of human interactions, of political malfeasance, of social discord, and of economic manipulation. Furthermore, the fact that the young man's father was 'light, bright, and damn near white' did little to insulate him from the horrors of his multiracial identity as a Black man in America.

Dr Christian examines how dubious theories emerged in the West that stigmatised peoples of mixed racial heritage. He also discusses how the 'one-drop rule' in the US established all people with a drop of African blood as 'Black'. Moreover, similar to his respondents' experiences, he exposes the social history, the validity and the tangible reality that this theory is still operating. In gathering primary sociological data from the city of Liverpool, England (which has arguably the oldest Black settlement in Europe), and having travelled and conducted further research in South Africa, Jamaica and the US, Dr Christian's study is well-informed. In this sense he provides a solid example of the 'indigenous researcher' who is keenly aware of the subtle nuances, of both verbal and body language, in providing a transcultural context for understanding the global characteristics of these specific multiracial identities. In point of fact his approach to this subject reflects what Linda Tuhiwai Smith calls for in her work, *Decolonizing Methodologies: Research and Indigenous People.* As she maintains:

Indigenous methodologies are often a mix of existing methodological approaches and indigenous practices. The mix reflects the training of indigenous researchers which continues to be within the academy, and the parameters and common sense understandings of research which govern how indigenous communities and researchers define their activities.[1]

Therefore Dr Christian's approach is clearly a 'mix' of sociological methods (mainly qualitative in scope) and 'indigenous'[2] common sense reflected in his engagement with respondents from several diverse age-groups within the Black British community. This indigenous approach is also borne out in the manner he has brought to us unique and relatively 'unheard voices' of the African diaspora. In using the US, South Africa and Jamaica as comparative case studies we are able to understand the global nature of multiracial identity constructs that were formed primarily under the umbrella of white supremacy. Dr Christian informs us about the 'hidden history' of multiracial identity and how both Africa and Europe have mingled beyond merely the confines of the 'oppressed and oppressor'.

The analysis of 'colourism' within the Black British experience is very important for two reasons. One, it broadens the discourse by examining the issue of colourism within the African world itself as it is situated at the source of European centredness. Two, as both premise and process, racialisation includes Europeans as well as non-European people of colour. Indeed, a clear understanding of the place in which these diverse people locate themselves allows for a richer analysis of racialisation and its human costs. In short, this study opens up new areas in an ethnographic sense.

Again to illustrate the complexity of multiracial and multicultural phenomena, my Catholic school experience showed me that the Irish and Italians are both European and Catholic but they are also culturally and biophysically distinct. Moreover, my West African sojourns as a social researcher have taught me that the Wolof, the Akan and the Igbo are also culturally and biophysically distinct. What galvanizes Europeans and their descendants as well as Africans and theirs are the political exigencies of the times and the shared cultural and cosmic norms that characterise them as unique human entities. Considered together, the purpose of racialisation as a social policy is expressed succinctly in the following:

The racialization of the human subject and the social order enable(s) comparisons to be made between the 'us' of the West and the 'them' of the Other.... This notion is also linked to Hegel's master–slave construct which has been applied as a psychological category (by Freud) and as a system of social ordering.[3]

Clearly Dr Christian's study shows the psychological impact of racialisation and, no doubt to the contestation of postmodernists, the fixation on the social ordering within the context of white Europeans and people of colour. He also explains how 'divide and rule' manifests itself in the maintenance of the status quo and white supremacy. The racialisation process also makes it easier to demarcate people of colour from one another.

From an African world perspective, multiracial identities are inclusive by definition. In fact, what makes Pan-Africanism a reality is based more on cultural and political affiliations than on skin colour and phenotype. Both continental and diasporan Pan-Africanists embody the casualties of white supremacy and racial hierarchies globally, and in its cultural and political activism it attempts to counter the psychological and physical terrorism associated with extreme right-wing behaviours and policies. The global structural realities of European-based hegemony differ according to the relative local realities of white numerical power and political/cultural histories. However, and in line with Dr Christian's analysis, the unifying force affecting all communities of colour, be they multiracial or not, is their relative inaccessibility to real power. Often it is power that not only determines the identities but also the economic and political tools necessary for their survival. Again, as Dr Christian precisely points out, the real problem of white supremacy is not so much its own self-denial, but its ability to socially engineer the tangible lives of human beings that it deems of lesser human value. Yet this self-denial and duplicity has the uncanny ability to eternally distance itself from the human disaster that it often creates.

In relation to multiracial identity, this research points out eloquently that from the eras of enslavement, colonialism, neo-colonialism to the present postmodern semantics, the human shuffling of the lower end of the pyramid has little or no impact on the eye of the pyramid. Interestingly, the few who control the many have become fewer in direct proportion to the world's population, while the many have become more racially diverse and inclusive of certain classes of whites, some by choice. Yet the horrific rise in racially motivated crimes is, and always has been, an outcome of the social scrambling at the bottom of the political and economic ladder. This is not to say that the structures and mechanism of white supremacy and hegemony are consistent globally. Indeed, who is white and, therefore, privileged varies markedly from one national setting to another – just as has been the case for multiracial persons globally. South Africa and Jamaica provide strident and dichotomous examples of the paradox of multiracial identity in the conundrum of this social phenomenon.

Where one fits and at what point of departure one may slip through the great racial divide in a global context reflects the irrational manifestation of white supremacist ideology in the first instance, and begs the question of its real purpose in the international social order. Dr Christian's research suggests that the global intellectual and activist communities of all hues should engage in this critical question. For ultimately, even the most distant member of the human family is, to use another sociological term, at risk.

Without doubt, this study is a unique contribution to scholarship and it illustrates the efficacy of a Pan-Africanist approach to an essentially sociological question. Rooted in the social history of conquest, subjugation and exploitation, the present everyday realities of multiracial and multicultural societies are not without connections from one part of the African descent world to another. In fact it is ahistorical and fundamentally flawed to discuss European hegemony in global terms without also discussing its global impact on peoples of colour, both intraculturally and interculturally. The validity of this approach is apparent in the responses of his informants to the intragroup colour conflict, and this directly correlates to the relative positions of privilege and access in either the US, UK, South Africa or Jamaica. The collective psychic trauma of African descendant peoples, whether on or from the African continent, along with those born in the African diaspora, are the unresolved consequences of highly racialised socio-political engineering and our collective socio-psychological trauma. The responses from the city of Liverpool, England, informants are highly enlightening and make clear the breadth of racial consternation within the African world community. Therefore this innovative research offers a necessary sociological approach to an all-African question. By extension, any of the external African diasporan cultures can attest that the discrimination that they face is not due to their birthplace identity but rather their racial, that is, African identity. Accordingly, as Dr Christian concludes his work: 'all roads lead back to Africa', and I might add, they also lead to a collective African experience globally.

Outline of the book

A major aim of this book is to provide historical and sociological insight, based on primary and secondary data, in regard to multiracial identity constructs. Chapter 1 takes account of the various ways in which multiracial identity has been theorised in a Western context and gives an explanation for the social construction of mixed racial heritage social groups. Chapters 2 and 3 consider the views of mixed racial origin persons, spanning two generations, who are natives of the city of Liverpool. Based on in-depth interviews (January–July 1996), the respondents consider their racial origins and reflect on how they regard themselves in a racial sense (all names have been changed to ensure confidentiality). Chapter 4 briefly examines the South African and Jamaican constructs of multiracial social groups. In each society the reality of white supremacy emerges in the historical construction of these racially divided societies. Chapter 5 critically assesses multiracial identity in relation to the 1990s 'cult' of hybridity theories in academia. In general, there is a lack of an historical perspective that acknowledges the deep-rooted reality of multiracial identities. Especially those that have been socially constructed within a white supremacist order. Crucially, this book is an attempt to explain how multiracial identities have longevity, and that this is often missing in the contemporary 'hybridity theories' that abound in academia.

Chair
Dept. of Pan-African Studies
Kent State University

Notes

1 L. T. Smith, *Decolonizing Methodologies: Research and Indigenous Peoples* (London: Zed Books, 1999), p. 143.
2 The idea of 'indigenous' is usually reserved for non-European populations in non-European countries. It is, however, this definition of indigenous that extends to people of colour *within* European-based societies and in European-dominated nations that allows for the use and application of the term here. Finally, it is worth noting that Dr Linda Tuhiwai Smith herself acknowledges the role of Black world scholarship in the development of her work.
3 Smith, *Decolonizing*, p. 32.

Acknowledgements

I want to thank the many persons who have helped sustain my strength to engage in this study through either intellectual or institutional support, friendship or kin ties. In the UK, thanks to: Jo Campling, Cameron Laux, Dorothy Kuya, Wally Brown, Stephen Small, Ray Costello, Hakim Adi, Ankie Hoogvelt, Kathryn Dixon, Ray Quintal, Vic Christian, Adam Hussein, William Ackah, Nat Okoro, Tunde Zack-Williams, Ken Drysdale, Eric Lynch, Sakhile Sibanda, Father Austin, Ibrahim Thompson, Gloria Hyatt, Marie Charles, Jayne Holden, Shirley Tate, Mike O'Grady, Ola Uduku, Malcolm Cumberbatch, Wanda Thomas-Bernard, Kent Roach. I would also like to mention the students I have taught at Charles Wootton College, the University of Liverpool, and Liverpool Hope University College. Along with my colleagues at the Institute of Commonwealth Studies, University of London.

In the US, along with the Fulbright Foreign Scholarship board, thanks to: William 'Nick' Nelson, Jr., Diedre L. Badejo, William 'Bill' Little, Molefi K. Asante, Edward and Shirley Crosby, Allayne Barnes, Mwatabu Okantah, Francis Dorsey, Ike Newsum, James Upton, Jeff Montgomery and Siri Briggs-Brown. All the staff and students who know me from the Ohio State University, Department of Black Studies, and Kent State University, Department of Pan-African Studies. In South Africa, many thanks to Portia Langa from the University of Durban at Westville, along with the students I met in various discussion groups. In Jamaica, Professor Barry Chevannes, Dean of the Social Sciences; Stephaney Ferguson and other members of the Library staff at the University of the West Indies, Mona; Antonio Atkinson of the African-Caribbean Institute of Jamaica; Kevin Fung from the Gleaner Archives Library; staff at the National Library of Jamaica; and the members of my family who took care of me: Hugh and Gloria McNab, Trevor and Carrol Christian. I am indebted to you all. Lastly, I would like to give a special thanks to those individuals who allowed me to interview them. It was often an 'invasion' of their deepest inner thoughts and I am certain that this could not have been easy – many thanks to you all.

Glossary

This glossary is intended to help the reader understand more readily the various terms that have been, and are still, used in discussions, both oral and written, involving 'race mixing' in 'Western' and 'Western*ised*' societies. Over time, and in different parts of the world, various terms have been employed to describe a person of 'mixed *racial* origin'. In this sense, it is necessary to recognise in some form the fact that 'racial labels' are not only historically and regionally specific, they are also often incongruously socially defined *within* societies. In addition, they can be viewed as derogatory terms in one society and largely acceptable in another. It is also important to note the scientific fact that it is now largely regarded as a fallacy to discuss the idea of 'pure racial types'. Indeed 'racial types' are merely social constructs which have become deep-rooted in Western thought and vernacular to describe what amounts to phenotypical variance, such as skin colour or hair texture, rather than innate biological differences between humans. Below are some of the most common terms to have been employed to define a mixed origin person of African and white European descent. (This study is not primarily concerned with other permutations of 'mixed races'. However, some of the definitions below have been used to describe a person of Asian and white European descent, e.g. 'half-caste', as well as an African and white European mixture.) Finally, I will state in each definition whether or not, in my opinion, the term can be viewed as derogatory.

I do not claim that what follows is an exhaustive list of the terms employed to define persons of African and white European mixed origin descent. However, the list represents many of the popular 'racial' terms which are used, or were once used, by writers and commentators. More importantly, although one of the terms provided below was most frequently used by the respondents in this study to describe themselves ('Black British'), this phrase ordinarily has not been associated *officially* with persons of mixed origin descent in a British context. Therefore, in my opinion, the term 'Black British' alone validates the use of a glossary in this study, as it shows again how racial*ised* labels do differ over time and place relating to persons of mixed racial origin.

Biracial: a term that is more common in the US than any-where else in the Western world and refers to people who have parents from two socially defined 'races', such as a person who has an African father and white European mother; or a Japa-nese mother and African American father. The permutations can be endless. The guru of multiracial identity in the US, Maria Root, contends that the term 'biracial' also refers to those per-sons who could claim a parent from a socially designated 'race' (such as African) and one who has derived from two, three or more 'races'. As Root maintains: 'This use of biracial moves us away from requiring equal "fractions of blood" to recognise the prevalence of blending'.[1] In other words the term allows for a definition for the manifold array of 'race mixtures' that can be associated in a given person. It is not viewed as a derogatory term, but would probably be contested by some writers as being too 'all-embracing'.

Black: I employ the capitalisation of the word 'Black' in this research to emphasise the way it emerged in the 1960s as a major *symbol* of racial pride emanating initially from the US. 'Black' is much more than just a colour.

Black British: Due to the fact that the majority of the younger mixed origin respondents in this study opted to define them-selves under this term, I thought it was important to add it to the glossary. At the outset of this study, however, I would not have included the term: it was only after I had interpreted the in-depth interviews that I thought it was necessary to add the definition. In essence, I would describe it as a term which does not designate a person a specific 'colour'. Rather it signifies a particular racial consciousness and way of life that identify the person as 'not being white'. The term acknowledges the politi-cal consciousness that emerged in the 1960s in the US, with 'Black is Beautiful' and so forth.

Cape Coloured: refers to those persons born of African and white European ancestry in South Africa. It is a term which is used to separate mixed origin persons from those of African/Black, white European and the various Asian communities in South Africa.

Under the Apartheid regime the 'cape coloureds' were given some privileges over African/Black peoples. In this sense, they acted as an intermediate social group (along with the Asians) between the minority white Afrikaans and the majority indigenous African/Blacks. It is not regarded as highly derogatory, but it is a term that will no doubt be further contested by all Africans in South Africa during the new era of 'multiracial democracy'.

Coloured: a term which has been used in different regions of the world and, as such, can be described as highly problematic. For instance, it has been used in Britain and South Africa to define persons of mixed racial heritage. However in Britain it has also been used to refer to people of 'pure' African/Black heritage. In the US it has been used in both senses and for various socially defined groups 'other than white American'. It can be said at the dawn of the twenty-first century it is a term which is very much outdated and rarely used to define persons having any degree of African/Black heritage. However, the term 'people of colour', mainly a US term, is in common usage to define, again, all 'racial' groups 'other than white American'.

Creole: a term used in the former colonies of the Portuguese, French and Spanish in the 'New World' and the African continent. It has referred to those persons of 'pure' white European stock born *in* the colonies (in contrast to those born in Europe). The term has also defined persons of 'mixed racial origin', especially in the state of Louisiana, US. Finally, it has also been defined as a language in itself (or *patois*) which developed from a pidgin (various combinations of African, Caribbean, English, and other European languages). It is usually not deemed a derogatory term and is employed commonly to describe various 'mixed ethnic groups' in Africa, the Caribbean and US particularly.

Cross breed: a derogatory term which has usually been employed by pseudo-scientific racists to describe the 'mixing' of 'pure' human 'races'. It is also used interchangeably to refer to the 'cross-breeding' of animals. The term should be regarded as demeaning and avoided if defining mixed origin persons.

Half-breed: a term often used derogatorily, and confusingly, to designate persons of mixed origin descent. *Chambers English Dictionary* (1992) refers to a 'half-blood' person, a 'relation between those who have only one parent in common'. In the US the term has been used in a derogatory manner to refer to the offspring of a Native American Indian and a white European. The term can be seen as derogatory and should not be used to describe persons of mixed origin descent.

Half-caste: a derogatory term, still in use today, and first employed by white Europeans to describe a person of Asian (usually Indian) and white European descent. However, it has been used also to refer to other people of mixed racial background in different regions of the world. In Britain, and the city of Liverpool particularly, the term is associated with persons born of African (also African Caribbean and African American) and white British/European heritage. Therefore the term has distinctly changed from its original usage. In explaining this term further, it is necessary to break it down. 'Half' of something is 'one of two equal parts'. One of the definitions of the word 'caste' in *Chambers English Dictionary* is 'a social class in India: an exclusive social class'. The word 'caste' is also derived from the Portuguese word *casta,* meaning breed, race. And also the Latin word *castus,* meaning pure, unmixed. Therefore 'half-caste' can be seen as a term which relates to the notion of there being 'pure races' (half = to be an equal half of a particular 'racial type') who have a particular social status (caste = relating to one's social standing, originally in India). Under the British Empire, the term 'half-caste' took on particularly negative connotations whereby the person of mixed racial ancestry was regarded as a social inferior (see Gill 1995 and Young 1995). In regard to the city of Liverpool, I argue that the term 'half-caste' is an extremely 'loaded' term which has been handed down from British Imperial folklore, via India, and took on an extended negative definition, relating specifically to the indigenous mixed origin population who have African and white British/European ancestry. Finally, my study reveals that the majority of respondents I made contact with find the term 'half-caste' offensive. However, some respondents continue to use the term to define themselves.

Hybrid: refers to a person of mixed origin descent. It is usually deemed a term relating to the 'blending' of either 'races' and/or 'culture'. In present academic discourse it is closely associated with postmodernist and postcolonial articulations of the heterogeneous nature of 'culture and nation'. It is not viewed as a derogatory term within the contemporary academic scene. However, when the term is associated, in a synonymous sense, with 'half-caste', 'half-breed', and so forth, it should be avoided.

Hypodescent: refers to the notion that a person of mixed origin descent is 'fixed' to the 'racial group' of his/her heritage which has the least social status in the given society. Thus, in the US any person having any degree of African heritage (i.e. the 'one drop rule') would be considered a member of the African American community, which has historically been given the least in social status and privilege. This definition is paraphrased from Root.[2] The term is more of an explanation for a 'racial type' and should not be viewed as derogatory.

Interracial: refers to relationships 'between races', such as black and white persons dating and sexual intercourse between the two. The offspring of an 'interracial couple' will ordinarily be classified as of mixed origin heritage (or any of the various definitions for that person cited here). The term is very popular in the US, where there is a magazine, established in 1989, entitled *Interrace*, which covers issues and current debates relating to 'interracial dating' and 'children of a mixed racial background'.

Melange: is a term employed by those persons of mixed racial heritage who do not want to specify any particular 'race'. It is a French word found in use in the US. It is an ambiguous term and should be used with caution.

Mestizo: refers specifically to persons having Spanish and Indian racial heritages. Very common in the US where it also broadly refers to persons of Latino and European descent. Not seen as a derogatory term, but must be used with discretion.

Miscegenation: refers to interracial dating and sexual intercourse between persons of different socially constructed 'racial groups'. It derives from the Latin words *miscere* (to mix) and *genus* (race). Most commonly used in the US, where some states, such as Virginia, had anti-miscegenation laws in practice up to 1967. The term is neither popular nor viewed as highly derogatory.

Mixed blood: a term often used to describe persons of mixed racial heritage. Not as derogatory as 'cross-breed' or 'mongrel', however, due to the use of the word 'blood', it gives the clear and incorrect impression of the existence of *biologically distinct* human groups. Therefore it is a term that should be avoided if possible.

Mixed-breed: *see* cross-breed, mixed blood.

Mixed origin: refers to persons born from varied socially de-fined 'races'. I prefer this because it is a flexible term with no negative connotation. For example, one can prefix the term with a particular people, e.g. African, which gives you the definition: *African of Mixed Origin.* In this sense the 'African' heritage is seen as the dominant factor in one's 'racialised make-up', which is often the social reality of those persons living in Western societies and of mixed origin descent. Yet it does not ignore the fact that the person may have other 'ethnic origins' (e.g. white British/European). It is also, in my opinion, a more rel-evant term to use, as 'origin' relates to descent, heritage, ancestry and so forth.

Mixed parentage: refers to persons of mixed origin descent and is presently very popular among British writers wanting to de-fine this social group. However it should be used with caution as it can be confusing. For example, is not a person having a white French mother and a white English father a person of 'mixed parentage'? Indeed the term can take away the social reality of 'race' *per se*. However, it is not seen as a derogatory term and is widely used in Britain at present.

Mixed race: a popular term in use today to define persons of mixed racial heritage. It is a term usually associated with per-sons having a parent of African descent and one of white European descent. However, as there is no such thing scientifically as 'races', many writers do not use the term, regardless of its popularity. It is therefore a term which should be used with caution. It is not considered highly derogatory, but it is a problematic term.

Mongrel: mostly associated with the result of the interbreeding of dogs. However, racist organisations such as the Ku Klux Klan of the US have often used the term to define the outcome of 'racial mixing' between Africans and Europeans. This form of definition is used by the KKK in order to create a 'moral panic' in the 'white race'. It is a highly derogatory term and should be avoided if one is to define persons of mixed origin descent.

Monoracial: refers to those persons who claim to have derived from a single 'racial stock'. It is also used to classify people into 'individual' 'racial types'. It is a term to be used with caution as it is scientifically fallacious.

Mulatto: refers to the offspring of an African and a white European. It is a Spanish term in origin, defining a 'little mule' (usually the sterile offspring of a horse and a donkey). Mostly found in use in the US. Again, this term, because of its demeaning association with animals, should be viewed as derogatory. However, just as the term 'half-caste' is still employed by some people today, the same can be said for the term 'mulatto'.

Multiracial: refers to persons having a 'multi'-dimensional racial heritage. For example, it allows for a person who could claim Irish, African, Chinese, and Native American heritage. It can also be used to define those persons of 'biracial' or 'mixed racial' descent. Therefore it may be deemed 'all embracing' of the 'racial types' of humankind. This term is becoming increasingly popular in the US, and there is a movement to have it as a 'racial category' in the next US Census in 2000. It is seen by and large as a positive term to use.

Octoroon: refers to a person having one-eighth African heritage and seven-eighths white European. It is a term that is most common in the US. It should be regarded as a derogatory term, like 'half-caste', as it is scientifically spurious to suggest one can measure an eighth of a person in terms of his/her 'racial ancestry'.

Quadroon: similar to 'octoroon', it refers to a person having one-quarter African heritage and three-quarters white European. *Chambers English Dictionary* extends it to refer to 'any person or animal of similar ancestry'. Again, it should be regarded as a derogatory term and avoided if possible.

1
Theorising Multiracial Identity

In the 1990s the academy witnessed a strong interest in 'identity politics', particularly in the US, UK and broader Western
context.[1] This chapter will consider the term 'multiracial identity'.
It is a phrase which is becoming rather popular in the US largely
through the activities and scholarship of a multiracial pressure
group.[2] Defining the term 'multiracial identity' involves examining two concepts in one phrase. As we have a working definition
for 'multiracial' (see the Glossary), we can focus more here on
comprehending the concept of 'identity' *per se*; recognising,
however, that even though it is a slippery entity to define, it is
still necessary to have an understanding of what it actually refers
to. This is primarily for the purpose of gaining greater clarity in
relation to any discussion involving 'racial mixing'. After establishing a sociological definition for 'identity' we can then consider
the theoretical and historical dimension of mixed racial identity
discourse, specifically within a US and UK frame of reference.

Toward a definition of identity

Identity as a sociological concept has been defined as the search
for 'self' and how one relates to the broader social context. Writing
in the 1950s, the renowned sociologist C. Wright Mills suggested
that the individual in society cannot be separated from the history
and social milieu of her times. Accordingly, each person has
a particular biography/history that is played out over time
and place.[3] A more contemporary sociologist, David Newman,
offers another way of thinking about identity, and suggests that
it is:

1

our most essential and personal characteristic. It consists of our membership in social groups (race, ethnicity, religion, gender and so on), the traits we show, and the traits others ascribe to us. Our identity locates us in the social world, thoroughly affecting everything we do, feel, say, and think in our lives.[4]

According to Newman, identity is all-embracing and it is something that has great relevance in our everyday social realities as members of social groups. Identity is also described as a phenomenon of multidimensional scope. That is, it encompasses complex variables such as 'race' and ethnicity. In postmodern parlance, identity is somewhat akin to a jelly-like substance which moves somewhere else when one tries to press on it. To put it another way, it never seems to be able to stand still. If you press on or shape one aspect of identity, this can then shift the image or interpretation to something other than what one wanted to see, or expected to see, and understand. As postmodern theorists suggest, identity is never static, it is constantly on the move.[5]

If we concede, as probably many postmodern theorists would, that identity is too difficult, if not impossible to define, then why is it that so many seemingly distinct social groups exist? For instance, why is there a need for census data relating to the specific 'race' and ethnicity of a person/group? Even if the term 'race' itself is largely useless in a scientific sense,[6] why in modern technological societies does it have such profound social significance? In view of these basic questions, surely there is something tangible and 'real' about identity in a social sense. Rather than stating that identity is simply out of reach or indefinable, it could be useful to argue that identity is real in the social sense; and that it does have significant cultural importance in peoples' lives. Especially in Western societies that remain stubbornly framed by 'race' and are openly articulated in cultural dominance.[7]

Certainly identity should be regarded as fluid, just as culture itself is. However, just as the car may change over years in terms of its outer shell and style, fundamentally it still functions in the same manner as when it was invented over a hundred years ago. Of course some cars may now go faster than they did a hundred years ago, but we still ordinarily regard them as *cars*. They have a specific function in a modern technological society. The same can be said in relation to planes, trains and ships.

In a sense, then, it seems logical to treat identity as something that changes over time in relation to the development of a society and its social relations among peoples; yet it can also have a continuity of purpose. History informs us that this type of social development can be both positive or negative within a given society. For instance, take the historical experience of African Americans in terms of their 'collective name' as a social group in US history and culture. Their collective experience has involved the social process of enslavement, dehumanisation and second-class citizenship status. Moreover, on the macro or broader societal level, they have historically and officially been regarded as 'Negroes', 'Coloureds', 'Black Americans' and more recently 'African Americans'. Of course on a micro or personal level some African Americans may still prefer to identify themselves as 'Negro', 'Coloured' or something else. Accordingly, then, there should necessarily be both macro and micro level understandings of identity.

Although identity labels can and often do change, the underlying attribute remains defined very much in the same manner as it was originally formulated. Therefore, as a social group African Americans may at present collectively identify as such; none the less they can still be viewed as being connected to 'previous' racialised labels that have been associated with them. Again this suggests that aspects of identity do have real social consequences on an individual or group. It is futile to deem this logic something merely 'essentialist' or 'nationalistic'. Indeed it is confidently claimed here that there is a definite social identity experience in being considered a 'person of colour' in the US or UK. The experience may well differ from person to person or from group to group in the manner that it manifests itself, but there is a collective social reality to what is qualitatively different in being associated or defined as a 'white' person/group in Western societies.

Crucially, it is accepted here that as a concept, identity is highly complex and fluid. Nevertheless it does have major significance when it is connected to social phenomena, such as the definition or modality of what a 'woman', 'man', 'Black woman', 'white man' may or may not represent. This social reality is both obvious and endemic in most societies. So one could ask why it is that so many postmodern theorists have such a difficult time coming to terms with what it is to be 'Black', or rather a 'person of colour', in the US or UK? Of course identity is something which is mutable. Yet often once a person/ group has been negatively labelled, no matter how many euphemisms are employed to offset it as a negative label, usually it is the historical, *underlying* definition of it that takes precedence in the course of everyday social interaction in a given society.

For the purposes of clarity, then, a working definition of identity should acknowledge the dynamic aspect of it, yet this ought not to detract from the fact that identities do exist and are extremely significant in the social world. As has been eloquently suggested by Benedict Anderson, identities may well be imagined,[8] but they are still 'real' in the manner that they are manifested in the modern world.

The idea of essentialist identities is largely unpopular in current postmodern discourse. Yet even those ardent scholars who are steadfastly denying or earnestly contesting an essential 'Black subject'[9] paradoxically market their individual and collective works under distinctly 'Black' book titles.[10] In particular, it seems that this type of postmodern theorist of 'race' and ethnicity refuses to accept the *essential* nature of socially constructed identities in theoretical terms only. This is made somewhat more incongruous given the fact that they often cede to the 'identity of the market-place', but not it seems to authentic social 'Black identities'. It is a market-place where the seller seeks the buyer in often clearly defined and socially constructed 'social groups'. One rarely observes this connection between the personal and the broader social forces until we look for it. Crucially, it is difficult to escape the fact that we are part and parcel of a social world that is shaped by power relations and social identities. The focus here is on 'racialised identities' and the issue of multiracial identity.

Multiracial identity as a term in the 1990s

Multiracial identity as a phrase has largely come into prominence through the work of a pressure group that came into being in the US in the 1980s and has in the 1990s picked up momentum.[11] Along with the advocates of multiracial identity, there has been a growth in magazines promoting intermarriage. Among these publications emanating from the US are *Interrace*, *Biracial Child* and *New People*. However, one could argue that there is nothing actually 'new' about people who can claim to have a multiracial heritage. As Spencer states:

> Black people and white people had intermixed in Africa and Europe long before the New World – 'America' – was ever 'discovered.' Thus, Black was never purely black, and white was never purely white, and our uses of these racial designations has been merely relative.[12]

Writing from the perspective of the African American experience, Spencer implicitly suggests how it is intellectually erroneous to think of multiracial identity as a modern or late twentieth-century social phenomenon. Yet, in reading the works of the many writers who collaborated with Professor Root in *The Multiracial Experience*, it is clear that they do not have a firm grasp on the historical terrain involving interracial relations. This is especially so in assessing their collective analysis of the US experience.[13] Indeed the collaborative work of Root et al. can be described as an attempt to produce an almost 'arty', avant-garde, 'new people' for a twenty-first century US that is devoid of the present endemic racism and racialised labelling. The collective analysis is rather naive as it fails to take full account of the deep-rooted history of racism and its concomitant social exclusion in the US. Asante has described the increasing number of 'Black multiracial theorists' as postmodernists who are 'racing to leave the race'.[14] Drawing from the work of Spencer, Asante asserts:

> the *New People* and *Interrace* group attempt to minimize the effects of blackness by claiming that they are neither white nor black, but colored. The nonsense in this position is seen when we consider the fact that nearly 70 per cent of all African Americans are genetically mixed with either Native Americans or whites. The post-Du Bois and perhaps more accurately, the post-Martin Luther King, Jr. phenomenon of seeking to explode racial identity has two prongs: one is white guilt and the other is black self-hatred. In the case of interracial families one often sees the urgent need to provide the offspring with a race other than that defined by custom, tradition, appearances, and history.[15]

For Asante, the multiracial advocates do not employ a logical and historical understanding of 'race relations' in the US. In agreement with Asante's position, the sociologist F. James Davis suggests that the 'one drop rule' is still very much the main criterion for the social definiton of an African American. That is, to have any amount of African ancestry, no matter how small, has meant being socially assigned to the African American community. According to Davis, who was writing in the early 1990s, the 'one drop rule' is still firmly embedded within the Black community of the US.[16]

Even though the idea of a 'new people' appears to be erroneous, advocates of multiracial identity in the US continue to persist with developing a pressure group in order to promote its cause – the 'cause' being that there should be a distinct recognition of 'multiracial persons' in law. In view of this it is worth considering the longevity of theoretical assumptions regarding so-called 'mixed race' persons in the US and UK contexts.

Historical theories of 'mixed race' persons

Most writers tend to agree that the main body of literature to emerge relating to mixed racial origin identity has come from the US;[17] beginning, arguably, in the late 1920s with the work of Robert E. Park, the renowned 'Chicago School' sociologist.[18] Park linked human migration and the social interaction of different peoples (e.g. Africans and white Europeans), producing an offspring that was in effect a 'marginal man.'[19] Theorising mixed racial origin identity in general, Park stated:

> Ordinarily the marginal man is a mixed blood, like the mulatto in the United States or the Eurasian in Asia, but that is apparently because the man of mixed blood is one who lives in two worlds, in both of which he is more or less a stranger.[20]

For Park the 'mixed blood' experiences a high degree of self-consciousness through being an alienated human being, who neither belongs to the white world nor the black world. Indeed he is deemed a 'stranger', an outcast or marginalised person in Western society. Park further suggests that it 'is in the mind of the marginal man that the two conflicting cultures (Black and white) meet and fuse'.[21] He theorised identity conflict as a dialectical and psychological process whereby 'the process of civilisation may best be studied'.[22] That is, paradoxically, the marginal man holds the key to our understanding of human progress, even though he lives a life of supposed 'inner conflict' and outer oppression from the social forces at large in the dominant society.

In addition, Park theoretically suggests that the person of mixed racial origin descent, born into societal structures that place an emphasis on maintaining racial distinctions, is caught up between conflicting racial ancestry. Because they cannot apparently claim full membership to neither the black nor the white worlds, mixed origin persons supposedly suffer from a psychological 'malaise'. Park contends that infused in the hereditary make-up of mixed origin persons is the 'low' (black) and 'high' (white) cultures; further, that this amalgamation brings forth the 'process of civilisation'. Yet, for Park, regardless of the seemingly 'positive' genetic and cultural dialectic, the person of mixed ancestry is still to be deemed 'psychologically maladjusted'.

This theoretical formulation for understanding the social and psychological condition of mixed origin persons, in modern societies such as the US and UK of the 1920s and 1930s, is substantiated in the work of another sociologist, Cedric Dover. He actually decries the social imagery of mixed origin persons as it appeared in the rather harsh and graphic language characteristic of the time in which he was writing:

> The 'half-caste' appears in a prodigal literature. It represents him, to be frank, most as an undersized, scheming and entirely degenerate bastard. His father is a blackguard, his mother a whore. His sister and his daughter, dressed by Coward and Cochran in a 'shimmering gown', follow the maternal vocation.

He continues: 'But more than all this, he is a potential menace to Western civilization, to everything that is White and majusculed.'[23] Dover notes with regret that at the time of his writing (1930s) probably the majority of theorists or social philosophers writing on the subject of interracial relationships and miscegenation believed that:

all hybrids are the work of the devil, that they inherit the vices of both parents and the virtues of neither, they are without exception infertile, unbalanced, indolent, immoral and universally degenerate.[24]

Judging by the work of Park and the critical insights of Dover there is little doubt that the 1920s and 1930s theorists on mixed origin social identity by and large perceived persons of this 'human-type' an aberration. A leading colleague and contemporary of Park, Everett V. Stonequist, also theorised the 'racial hybrid' as a marginal person beset with inner conflict and disharmonious attributes.[25] However, another sociologist, Dickie-Clark, later suggested that Stonequist had confused the concept of marginality, and emphasised presumed psychological characteristics instead of focusing on how it is the inevitable outcome of a marginal situation *within* a given society.[26] Dickie-Clark argues that Stonequist's overall analysis does not clearly state what it is exactly that makes the so-called 'racial hybrid' a distinctly marginal person.[27] The questions we should ask are: is it a psychological effect of being the product of a 'Black' person and a 'white' person, within a framework of cultural and genetic conflict? Or is it *Society* itself creating the marginal person?

Given this lack of theoretical clarity concerning the concept of marginality, it makes sense to seek the views of mixed origin persons themselves in order to ascertain how they view themselves within their given social surroundings (Chapters 2 and 3 cover this with a case study of Liverpool in the UK). In providing a methodology that encompasses both a theoretical and empirical base we are more able to comprehend the *subjective* opinions of mixed origin persons. This in turn complements a theoretical analysis that covers the historical and contemporary social backdrop. In addition, this can aid in the determination as to whether or not the individual of mixed origin descent actually, in an empirical sense, reflects the theoretical 'racial hybrid' type put forward by Park, Stonequist and other sociological theorists of mixed racial identity. Crucially, this also allows the theoretical space to consider other possibilities of 'marginality' that may exist in a society's cultural make-up – rather than, as has been presumed, it being a product of congenital or internal conflict.[28] It could well be shown that there is a man-made stigmatisation process whereby persons of mixed origin descent have been unjustly labelled 'psychologically maladjusted'.[29]

Indeed, historically, major world societies have adopted 'colour-caste' situations (e.g. in the US under Segregation Laws; in Jamaica under British Colonialism; and in South Africa under the Apartheid system) whereby social groups were stratified in a hierarchy relating to social prestige and acceptability. This was often solely related, somewhat incongruously, to phenotype characteristics. That is, with white at the top, brown, red and yellow skinned peoples occupying the middle and dark-skinned Blacks being situated at the bottom. This had significant consequences for a social group's self-perception and world-view in coming to an understanding of themselves or the 'self'. Janet E. Helms argues persuasively that racial categorisation in this manner can often be used erroneously to mean 'racial identity'. As she states:

> the term 'racial identity' actually refers to a sense of group or collective identity based on one's *perception* that he or she shares a common racial heritage with a particular racial group.[30]

This begs the question: how do we come to develop our 'perceptions' of sharing a common racial heritage? Again, one way of attempting to put meat on this skeleton-like question is to examine the historical experience of those who may have been socially constructed as a distinct 'racial group', as in the case of mixed origin persons in South African history. The 'Cape Coloureds' certainly fit the characteristics of a 'man-made' social group in the history of South Africa. In putting an emphasis on the social construction of 'racial types' this case diminishes the tendency to erect willy-nilly and anomalous categories of mixed origin persons, especially when they are socially constructed in a manner that deems them somehow fixed or absolute. In regard to this study, what is required is a better way for understanding how persons of mixed origin descent have historically been *pathologically theorised*.

Writing from a UK perspective on mixed origin identity, Ann Phoenix and Barbara Tizard point to the theoretical work of both Park and Stonequist in the 1920s and 1930s and state: 'it is important to realise that the theory was not supported by empirical investigations. It was presumably based on personal observations.' They continue: 'No such studies were made in the United States or elsewhere of racially mixed people. Nevertheless, the belief that they will almost inevitably experience a divided self, with consequent psychological problems ... has been widely accepted.'[31]

Tizard and Phoenix were incorrect to suggest that no empirical studies were carried out 'elsewhere'. Indeed, the present research reveals that a sociological investigation was carried out in Liverpool, England between 1928 and 1930 regarding the 'half-caste' problem in the city. This is a notorious report, and since it does not have extensive recognition outside the city of Liverpool it deserves consideration as a primary source in UK multiracial studies.[32]

Nevertheless, as Tizard and Phoenix have suggested, by and large studies in the 1940s continued to theorise mixed origin persons as anomalous outcasts. For instance, in the 1940s, the works of the noted sociologists Wirth and Goldhamer, and Gunnar Myrdal, each drew negative conclusions regarding the social and psychological condition of 'mixed bloods'. Moreover, they acknowledged the growing antipathy toward Black–white sexual relations in the US.[33] Wirth and Goldhamer did, however, point out the relatively similar socially stratified position that both 'light-skinned' and 'dark-skinned' African Americans held at the time of their study. Returning to the concept of the 'marginal man' they suggested:

It is important to recognise ... that in a sense *every* Negro, whether light or dark, is a marginal man in American society; for this reason, also, one might expect that the personality of the light-coloured Negro would not deviate in too marked a degree from that of his 'co-racialist.'[34]

The argument put forward by Wirth and Goldhamer runs in line with the 'one drop rule' and the analysis of Professor Davis above. That is, regardless of how 'white' a person may look in appearance, if he/she is known to have any amount of African heritage this is criterion enough for the person to be classified as an African American. This form of racial stratification was constituted in the majority of state legislatures, and effectively it was a *de jure* enforcement of the 'one drop rule'.[35]

In point of fact Davis cites a case in 1948 Mississippi where a light-skinned African mixed origin man received a severe jail sentence:

David Knight, was sentenced to five years in jail for violating the anti-miscegenation statute. Less than one-sixteenth black, Knight said he was not aware that he had any black lineage, but the state proved his great-grandmother was a slave.[36]

Incidents of this sort make the task of trying to 'theorise' about so-called 'mixed bloods' or 'mulattos' all the more complex in a society such as the US. Indeed, as mentioned above, fundamentally in the historical sense the federal government and state legislatures have viewed all persons having claim to an African heritage as 'Negro', 'Coloured', 'Black' and/or more recently 'African American'. Yet this overtly contradictory situation shows how on the one hand a person has an idea of his or her 'raciality', but on the other the social forces of the society's law-making bodies deem this 'personal sense of the racial self' irrelevant.

The situation of David Knight, in 1948 Mississippi, who 'didn't know he was black', and presumably thought and acted as a White person, is a clear example of the complexity involved in racialised labelling. Knight was prosecuted for 'acting white' after the state claimed he was an African American. This situation is not fantasy, but profoundly real in the social sense. It is not something hypothetical or imagined. It is a genuine social experience of being regarded as 'Black' in a society structured historically by racial stratification. One could add that this example is from a past era and that it is something foreign in the US in the late 1990s. However, race relations are still a major problem in the US and only a fool could suggest that if a person is known to have 'one drop' of African heritage, it could be of no significance in his/her social existence.

Contemporary US theories in multiracial identity

Given the reality of the 'one drop rule', it is somewhat strange that back in the 1940s Wirth and Goldhamer were theorising that it was more likely for 'mixed bloods' in later generations not to regard themselves as a distinct group in the US.[37] They argued that the 'destiny' of mixed origin persons would largely be dependent on the broader African American community's social development. In other words, African mixed origin persons would be fully 'assimilated' into the majority Black community and the *shade* of their skin *within* it would become insignificant.

To a large extent Wirth and Goldhamer were correct in their assessment of this aspect of the African American experience. Indeed, more than fifty years on, both light-skinned and dark-skinned African Americans are *legally* regarded in society as a homogeneous social group. However, with over 50 years of hindsight, evidence contradicts their prediction of a totally unified African American community in terms of 'racial identity' structure and consciousness.[38] In point of fact Spickard contends that the 'one drop rule' no longer applies. In attempting to defend his position he states:

> before the last third of the twentieth century, multiracial individuals did not generally have the opportunity to choose identities for themselves [in the US]. In the 1970s and particularly in the 1980s, however, individuals began to assert their right to choose identities for themselves – to claim belonging to more than one group, or to create new identities.[39]

Spickard is supported by the multiracial pressure group in the US and many other writers in his field of enquiry.[40] There is a problem with his perspective, as he describes himself as a 'white mongrel European American' and leaves us with little doubt that he is not entirely aware of the derogatory history, in the racial sense, of a word such as 'mongrel'. Spickard may well be endeavouring to 'neutralise' this term, but his attempt comes across as rather facile and supercilious.[41] To put it another way, as a 'white mongrel European American' he has the privilege of mocking the social reality of 'minority racial labels' as he can always slide back into his 'White racialised ethnicity' whenever he chooses. This is not the case for those persons who are distinctly or in part 'Black'.

Taking Spickard's argument further, Root suggests that the repeal by the Supreme Court in 1967 of anti-miscegenation legislation in the US signals a demarcation between the 'old' and 'new' ways of theorising and researching the life experience of mixed origin persons.[42] She further states that the 'old literature' described mixed origin persons as 'deviant' in an era characterised by 'linear theorising' and 'rigid racial boundaries'. Moreover, the old literature was bolstered by the 'combined forces of pseudoscience and moralistic theology'.[43]

If the 'old literature' is considered negative and pathologising of mixed origin persons, contemporary theorists, mainly in the US, have responded by creating a 'new literature' that categorises mixed origin persons basically as a 'separate entity'. Along with this literature, the multiracial pressure group have protested in the US to have a special 'multiracial' category placed in the Census by the year 2000.

Yet having spent over four years researching the isssue, the US Office of Management and Budget (OMB) stated in October 1997 that there would be no 'multiracial' category in the 2000 census forms.[44] In addition, civil rights groups were anxious as to how federal agencies would tabulate a 'multiracial' category in terms of the Voting Rights Act, as this ensures that Black and other minorities are democratically represented. As a result of this worry, even if a person decides to tick herself as 'Black' and another 'race' on the 2000 census form, she will *still* be regarded as African American.[45] The compromise means at bottom that a person of mixed racial heritage can tick as many boxes as he or she pleases, but if one of the 'ticks' represents 'Black' or 'African American' the individual will be ultimately acknowledged as such in a racial and social sense. Again, in terms of US governmental racial classification for 2000, this appears to indicate the deep-rootedness of the 'one drop rule' and its continuance in stratifying the African American community.

Before the OMB decision in October 1997 the multiracial pressure group was optimistic about creating a 'new people'. As Christine Hall suggested in 1996:

> The future . . . points to the reality of a *formal* multiracial identity. In additon to mixed-race people experiencing simultaneous membership in various ethnic/racial groups, they are also acknowledging themselves in the new category of *multiracial.* [my italics][46]

It appears that this optimism was premature and out of place in a real world of social identities that are shrouded in racial classification. The US is a society that is profoundly and historically embedded in racial consciousness. Members of the multiracial pressure group clearly underestimate this reality.

Indeed, for basic political reasons an argument has been put forward explaining that multiracial advocates are 'splintering' the African American community by pushing for a multiracial category. Rather than being positive, this action could simply prove detrimental for all concerned. In an article written by Michael K. Frisby for *Emerge,* not long before the OMB made its decision, he cites Professor William Strickland, who states intelligently, prophetically and unreservedly:

> It's understandable that people want to honor both their parents, but politically it is deleterious. Even though we may define ourselves in a certain way, the system does not . . . It's silly to pretend that this system [in the US] doesn't see us all as niggers.[47]

Theorising mixed origin identity in the US will no doubt continue to raise heated debates. The goal that the multiracial pressure group is pushing for is far from being achieved in the near future. This is due mainly to the intransigence of the 'one drop rule' that has governed the social identity of *all* African Americans. Certainly this has been the situation since the Declaration of Independence was signed in 1776, and arguably this was the case under British colonialism.[48]

Contemporary UK theories of multiracial identity

Theories of mixed origin identity in the UK context are limited due to the relative scarcity in scholarship specifically relating to the subject. Nevertheless there has been a degree of comparative analysis with the US experience.[49] A reason for the lack of studies in the UK relating to mixed origin identity may be found in the fact that the 'ethnic minority' population accounts for only 5.5 per cent of the overall population figure and the 'mixed' racial categories of 'Black-other' and 'Other-other' represent less than 1 per cent, according to the 1991 Census. Table 1.1 shows the 'racial' breakdown of the UK population. In terms of persons being categorised as 'Black mixed', we can only speculate that this is under the categories of 'Black-other' and 'Other-other'. 'Black-other' accounts for 178,401 persons and 'Other-other' accounts for 290,206 persons, which equals 0.8 per cent of the population.

Together these two racial categories account for a potential 468,607 persons of mixed origin identity in the UK; that is, excluding the 'Other-Asian' category. Therefore there are approxi-

Table 1.1   The ethnic composition of Britain's population, from the 1991 Census[54]

Ethnic Group	Number	%
White	51,837,794	94.5
Black Caribbean	499,964	0.9
Black African	212,362	0.4
Black-other	178,401	0.3
Indian	840,255	1.5
Pakistani	476,555	0.9
Bangladeshi	162,835	0.3
Chinese	156,938	0.3
Other Asian	197,534	0.4
Other-other	290,206	0.5
Total ethnic minority population:	**3,015,051**	**5.5**

mately half a million mixed origin persons in the UK with a degree of African heritage. However, we can be more certain of the 'Black-other' racial category, giving us near the 20 per cent of a million figure, than we can be of the 'Other-other'.

There are a number of issues related to this 'racial categorisation' which are pertinent to this study. First, the government data in the UK relating to racial classifications are extremely nebulous and fail to give a clear definition of what a person actually is in terms of their specific racial origins. Indeed, what does 'Black-other' particularly tell us about a person? Even more inexplicable is the term 'Other-other'. Robert Moore, who is an expert in UK 'race relations' has made clear the vagueness of this term in rather satirical fashion, stating that it could basically be described to 'anything' from a Martian to an Everton football supporter.[50] It is difficult to disagree with this assessment, as a number of the above racial classifications are indeed, at best, crude and certainly lacking in terms of racial clarification.

The few studies that have emerged relating to mixed origin identity in the UK have focused primarily on 'mixed relationships' and their offspring.[51] Other writers on 'mixed racial' identity such as Wilson, and Tizard and Phoenix, specifically focused their studies on mixed origin identity among children below and up to adolescence.[52] Wilson conducted her study in the late 1970s and drew a sample of 51 children of mixed origin descent (having either an African or African Caribbean and white British parent) aged between 6 and 9 years; while Tizard and Phoenix interviewed 58 teenagers of a similar 'racial type' aged between 15 and 16 years.[53] Each of these studies reached an opinion that a 'mixed origin identity' was asserted by many of their respondents and concluded that it was wrong to suggest that mixed origin children would necessarily be 'confused' or 'psychologically maladjusted' in reference to their identity. In regard to this Wilson in her study states:

> Contrary to the popular stereotype of mixed race people as torn between black and white, many children seem to have found a happy and secure identity for themselves as 'black mixed race'.[55]

However, Wilson did emphasise the word *black* in line with 'mixed race' and stated that she did not want, unlike many writers in the contemporary US, to suggest that the mixed origin children she studied ought to be seen as somehow 'separate' from the broader Black community.[56] On the contrary, she asserts that 'mixed race' children should be proud of their 'Blackness' and set it at the core of their identity structure. Her logic for this position is to argue that, whether one is light-skinned or dark-skinned, as a designated 'Black person' racial discrimination in British society is by and large the same for both. Nevertheless, Wilson states that on a personal level, it does no harm to recognise the fact that these children are of 'dual heritage,' and acknowledging the fact themselves that they have a degree of 'white heritage' should not cause them 'psychological pathology'.[57]

In their study, Tizard and Phoenix state that about 60 per cent of their sample of mixed origin teenagers saw themselves as being of 'mixed race'. While 20 per cent were regarded as an intermediate group, not being troubled by their 'Blackness', 20 per cent of the sample were regarded as having 'identity problems' of the 'marginal man' variety.[58]

Collectively these studies have proved useful in articulating the views of mixed origin children and given a much needed insight into the complexities of how *they* see themselves in a society such as the UK which has been regarded as a 'white man's country'.[59] One cannot underestimate the significance of Britain's colonial past, ingrained with a racist ideology and the myth of white supremacy. In addtion it is in this context that interracial sexual relations were both condemned *and* condoned.[60]

A problem for the die-hard racist is that a person of mixed origin descent represents a living defiance to his warped racist outlook – as in her very existence she contests the notions of white supremacy and 'pure races' – such as the 'Aryan Myth'.[61]

Although this study does not concern itself specifically with the issue of 'transracial adoption', it is useful to briefly point out a debate within social work in the UK regarding the identity of 'mixed race' children and the adoption procedure. A prominent Black writer in social work policy, John Small, has argued persuasively that mixed origin children should be identified as 'Black' by families who adopt them.[62] They should also be in close touch with Black culture and Black people. In other words, there should be no distinction made between those children who have none, one or two Black parents in the UK. Small's opinion is that mixed origin children are essentially seen as 'Black' in the UK, and to think of themselves as anything else would have an adverse affect on their self-esteem and identity. This is a contested issue, as it has been suggested that 'mixed race' children do not necessarily have a negative conception of themselves.[63] Small, however, is of the opinion that mixed racial origin children (those of African/African Caribbean and white British European descent) should be regarded as 'Black' in a social reality sense; and he particularly does not agree with the term 'mixed race'. As he states:

> The concept of mixed race, which has become part of conventional social work language, is misleading because it causes confusion in the minds of transracial adopters. It can lead them to believe that such children are racially distinct from other blacks. Consequently, they may neglect the child's need to develop a balanced racial identity and thereby a well integrated personality. The term 'mixed race' should therefore not be used by administrators or professionals, and should be discouraged among people who provide homes for black children. Many black people find the term derogatory and racist because they feel it is a conscious and hypocritical way of denying the reality of a child's blackness. Certainly, mixed-race children are regarded as black by society and eventually the majority of such children will identify with blacks, . . . It is therefore more appropriate to use the term 'mixed parentage' instead of 'mixed race'.[64]

According to Small, being of mixed origin descent is no different from being 'Black' in the UK societal sense.[65] He emphasises
the role 'society' plays in shaping the modality of 'race and
ethnicity' which overrides the specific racial make-up of the
individual: not being white makes you Black, regardless of the
amount of African ancestry one may possess. Nick Banks, another writer in the area of social work, implicitly supports the
view of Small and argues that those in the UK having the power
to define society's racial labels often means that the individual's
opinion of 'self' has limited mileage in the labelling process.
As Banks points out:

> The selection of ethnic identity as a form of allegiance to a
> particular group cannot be chosen. It is imposed by those
> who wish to keep safe the highly guarded frontier between
> black and white. Being of mixed ethnicity poses a threat to
> the purity of those with the power and motivation to guard
> this frontier.[66]

For Banks and Small, 'racial identity' is largely imposed by
the social forces prevalent in society. They each put forward a
macro perspective on the structural imposition of racial*ised* identity
in the UK context. This is a perspective that is in some ways
different from the position taken by Tizard & Phoenix and
Wilson,[67] who in their studies look particularly at the micro
aspect of 'mixed racial identity' constructs. Arguably, the key
point in theorising multiracial identity is to note how social
theorists have tended to focus on either macro or micro determinants. However, a more productive task would be to understand
the implications of both.

Conclusion

In sum, theorising 'mixed race' or 'multiracial' identity is fraught
with conceptual complexities. Yet what can be suggested here is
that it is certainly an issue of social significance given the continued prevalence of 'racialised relations' in modern societies
such as the UK and US. Therefore it would be incorrect to ignore this social reality due to the probems of conceptualising
and theorising this global phenomenon. This chapter has covered some of the key theoretical themes relating to multiracial

identity. The following two chapters examine the personal views of mixed racial origin respondents. The interviews took place in Liverpool, England in 1996. In providing the everday thoughts of respondents having parents of both African and European descent, my main aim is to marry theoretical themes with 'every-day' insight into this social phenomenon.

2
Speaking for Themselves (I): *Definitions of the Racial Self and Parental Influence*

> In these postmodernist times the question of identity has taken on colossal weight particularly for those of us who are post-colonial migrants inhabiting histories of diaspora.[1]

This chapter will consider the ways in which 20 gender-balanced 'mixed race' respondents from two generations make sense of themselves as persons of dual, African and European, ancestry. The interviews took place in the city of Liverpool, England in 1996. All the respondents are natives of the city of Liverpool and have lived most of their lives there. The definitions of 'self' and 'parental influence' are the two key themes. The responses to the theme of how they describe themselves is important. Yet the influence of the parental line is also significant in understanding how 'mixed race' persons come to view themselves in the social world. A main objective of the interviews was to allow the respondents' own words to take prominence in the discussion. This strategy was to serve as a way of empowering them to 'speak for themselves'.

Embedded within the two themes is a discussion as to whether the subjective experience of social identity formation has in any manner been influenced by broader social forces at play in society, in particular the racialised value systems that emanate from both 'Black and white worlds'. However, before we take account of the mixed racial origin respondents' views, it is first necessary to provide a short history of Black settlement in the city of Liverpool.

Black settlement in the city of Liverpool, UK

The city of Liverpool is located in the north-west of England and is noted for being the home of arguably the world's most famous pop group: the Beatles. Yet, although it is far less publicised, the city is also noted for its long-established Black settlement in the South End dockland area. Due to the city's seafaring links with West Africa and the Caribbean during the era of the Atlantic slave trade and beyond, and the two world wars, many Black seamen, soldiers, munition workers and students settled in the city and married or cohabited with local white women.[2] As such, there has developed a mixed racial origin community which spans several generations. Although as a social group they were often in official circles described as 'half-castes', since the 1960s they have been largely referred to in the colloquial sense as 'Liverpool-born Blacks'. They have a significant presence in the city, and according to the 1991 census figures make up the largest group in the Liverpool Black community. In relation to their socio-economic standing, 'Liverpool-born Blacks' have also been characterised as experiencing major structural racial discrimination that is 'uniquely horrific' compared to that faced by other Black communities across the UK.[3]

Another key aspect in the history of Black settlement in the Liverpool 8 or Toxteth area of the city relates to arguably the worst disturbances on mainland Britain during the 1981 'riots' or 'uprisings' that occurred across Black communities in Britain.[4] Since 1981 numerous community development initiatives have been put in place in Toxteth in order to provide the necessary socio-economic regeneration of the area. Yet much of the inner-city poverty remains a feature of the social landscape, that which is characterised by the high unemployment of 'Liverpool-born Blacks'.[5] This is the social backdrop that accompanies the views of the two generations of 'mixed race' respondents below. In short, they have each emerged from a rather deprived environment, and from one that is regarded as particularly horrific in a racial discriminatory sense.

How the Liverpool respondents define themselves in a racial sense

a) The older men (born between 1925 and 1945)

Much of our personal understanding of 'who we are' often rests on how in fact we each define ourselves in a racial sense. The discussion in Chapter 1 relating to the theorisation of mixed racial identity revealed the complexity of racial labels. We have considered how difficult/it is to define persons of mixed racial heritage through, for example, census data forms, and it was suggested that a study of the subjective mixed origin experience can help clarify our understanding at the micro-personal level. In addition, having two sets of generational cohorts of mixed origin adult persons who have been born and raised in the city of Liverpool, gives a historical dimension and allows a specific case study. In turn, this may help explain how racial labels are certainly not fixed entities but in fact can change over time and place.

Among the 'older men' respondents, when asked how he defined himself in a racial sense, Ian Taylor, aged 64, said: 'I'm very proud to be Black, I'm proud to be Igbo. I can't say I'm not proud to be English, because I am.'

When I pointed out to Ian that he had earlier informed me that his mother was of Scottish descent and, therefore, why did he now refer to himself as part 'English', he stated: 'Well, I was never brought up in Scotland and as far as I know my mother wasn't either.' This is an interesting point to his definition of 'self' in a racial sense, as he puts an emphasis on *region* or where he was born and raised in relation to what he has inherited *racially* from his mother. In this respect her being of Scottish descent is irrelevant: for him she's now 'English' having been born and raised in Liverpool, England. In contrast, in terms of what he has inherited 'racially' from his father, he has neither been to Nigeria nor been raised in terms of a specific African culture, but he is still 'proud to be an Igbo and a Black man'. For Ian, unlike his mother's place of origin, his father's place of origin has a deep psychological significance for him and it is highly relevant to him in terms of his sense of 'self'. When I pointed out this apparent contradiction to him he stated:

We're talking about skin now, we're talking about skin. I couldn't walk down [the street] and say I'm white, my mam's white, I can't do that. What I can do is be proud of my mother's skin, be proud that she was my mother. And still be proud, cos she borne me no matter what her skin colour is. I turned out this way [Black], it doesn't mean I can have disrespect [for his mother].

It appeared in the interview that Ian had a deeply felt respect for his mother. However, in terms of the social reality of his existence, he also knew that he was generally regarded as a Black person in British society. He was certainly proud of his African heritage in so far as his identity of origin (West Africa) had profound relevance to him, unlike his mother's 'white heritage' relating to Scotland. Interestingly, Ian did not find the term 'half-caste' offensive, though he did not use it to describe himself.

Harry Fredricks, again in his sixties, defined himself variously as both 'Liverpool-born Black', 'Anglo African' and/or 'Black British'. He pointed out that as a child the term 'half-caste' was a familiar label to use, but neither he nor his mother liked to use it (his father died when Harry was only 4 years of age):

I've never been comfortable with 'half-caste', even as a kid. Even as a child for some reason. My mother never liked the term 'half-caste'. She didn't stereotype like that, she'd say 'don't let them be calling you "half-caste" you know'. She was very sensitive to the negativity of the term. My mother told me most of my awareness of racism. She was very aware of it.

William Billing, a man in his fifties, was very emphatic in his definition of himself in a racial sense. He regarded himself proudly as a 'Liverpool-born Black' and for him it had great significance. Indeed his understanding of the term gave a further dimension to it which I had not encountered before in my interviews. I asked him to unpack the term 'Liverpool-born Black' for me and he stated:

I think it goes back to the problem in Liverpool where you had ... the initial term was 'half-castes' or the 'half-caste boys' ... They were the kind of terms we had when we were kids you know ... And so the 'half-castes'. So as we become more aware, that it was a bad term 'half-caste' . . . we said, no, we're not 'half-castes' man. We're Black, but we're not Caribbean Black. Because the Caribbean communities, themselves saw the Liverpool Blacks as trouble. As, as wild men. Or what they called the 'half-caste' boys out of control.

William appeared unwittingly to regard both 'Liverpool-born Black' and 'half-caste' as synonymous terms within the Liverpool context, and so I asked him whether he could define 'Liverpool-born Black': 'It's a way of saying that it's a Black person born in Liverpool whose probably got a white mother.'

I then prompted him a little further by saying that the term 'Liverpool-born Black' does not clearly state in logical English that the person identified as such ordinarily has a white mother. In reply he stated, 'it says you're a Black person born in Liverpool'. I then asked him why he saw the 'change' (albeit not by everyone at one particular time and place) in terminology from 'half-caste' to 'Liverpool-born Black'. He did not fully provide an answer but he did show the ambiguity of the term:

> Because I think 'half-caste' is really sort of saying your, there's a connotation, they're saying you're not a full person. You're half of something, not a full human being. You know the opposite to 'half-caste' was 'full-blood'. People would say well 'he's full-Black'. And they would think that if you're 'full-Black' you're better than being 'half-caste'. It's worked both ways really. It depends on how you see it. If it's a positive Black situation 'full-Black' is better than 'half-caste', better than white. Or it could be white's better than Black, and the 'half-castes' better than Black, better than the 'full-Black', do you know what I mean [he laughs]. It depends on where you stand really, it's nonsense really.

It is evident in William's understanding of the terms 'half-caste' and 'Liverpool-born Black' that ambiguity emerges. Nevertheless, no matter how unclear, his view can be corroborated. 'Liverpool-born Black' as a term is a euphemism for a much maligned and detested phrase: 'half-caste'. Identification with such a term as 'Liverpool-born Black' often indicates a sense of racialised consciousness in which a person, such as William, can articulate a distinct life experience. 'Liverpool-born Black' is certainly something unique to the city of Liverpool, as you do not hear terms such as 'Birmingham-born Black' or 'London-born Black', for example, elsewhere in Britain. Rather it appears to be a term created solely in the context of the Black experience in the city of Liverpool.

Stan Staunton, in his seventies, comfortably identified himself as a 'half-caste'. When asked to elaborate on why he defined himself in this manner he stated:

> I reckon it should be 'half-caste' because we're half and half aren't we? Well it doesn't really matter because we know we're Black, well we know we're not white because me skin's not.

He continued,

> I had a friend who was 'half-caste' and he didn't like that term Black. He didn't mind 'half-caste' . . . Because he knew he was half and half. His father was West Indian, his mother was white. So therefore it makes it halfy-halfy doesn't it? You can't argue with white cos your mother's white, you can't argue with Black cos your father's Black, so you're in-between aren't you?

Stan was literal in his understanding of what it was to be of mixed origin descent. He thought in terms of the white/Black dichotomy of their being distinct human 'races'. Stan considered himself as 'half and half' in one sense, yet still 'Black' in another, as he thought he would never be seen as 'white' in the eyes of society. What emerges from his understanding of his mixed racial origins is both a personal point of view and a pragmatic reality of his social condition. The personal point of view refers to the logic of his mixed racial descent; his understanding of the pragmatic reality notes that in the broader society he will ultimately be judged as being a 'Black man', or certainly of 'not being white'. Stan had no axe to grind with the term 'half-caste' and considered it the best term to use despite its unpopularity in the broader Black community. He was unaware of the negative meaning of the phrase and saw it as essentially harmless.

Chris Jones during the interview described himself as a 'Black man' without hesitation. However, in the questionnaire he had described himself as a 'half-caste'. This raises the issue of there being possible confusion of the terms for some respondents. Chris may in fact see the two terms, 'Black' and 'half-caste', as synonymous within the context of his life experience. It is not surprising to find some respondents using the racial labels interchangeably given the ambiguity and connotation of them within the context of the city of Liverpool.

b) The younger men (born between 1960 and 1975)

When asked how he defined himself in a racial sense, Terry Frost, a 20-year-old from the younger generation, stated: 'As a Black man, as a Black person I'm proud.' I asked him to relate his definition to the city of Liverpool context and he replied:

> I look at me-self like this, as far as I know and as far as I understand, ok yeah, I am born and raised in Liverpool, I am a scouser yeah, but where my culture and identity is concerned I just class myself as a Black.

For Terry, 'Black' had to do with 'culture and identity'. Being of mixed origin descent and where he was born and raised did not play a major role in his conceptualization of 'what it is to be Black'. He acknowledged the fact that he was born in Liverpool, he was a 'scouser', but his culture and identity are for him apart from that. He somehow distinguished between being born and raised in Liverpool and being 'Black'; they were essentially two different entities. When I asked him his thoughts on the term 'half-caste' he found the word very offensive and would never be associated with it. Again this may be deemed an aspect of his pride in being 'a Black man', that he is aware of his culture and identity in a positive sense. In other words, he identifies with the phrase 'Black is Beautiful' in terms of his racial consciousness and social development.

Adrian Jeffries is in his thirties and, as with Terry, found the term 'half-caste' offensive and would prefer not to be associated with it. When asked how he defined himself in a racial sense he stated: 'I put down in questionnaires "Black British". I'm light-skinned but I still class myself as Black.' I asked him why he classed himself as 'Black' given his acknowledgement that he is 'light-skinned'; he replied:

Because for me Black isn't a colour. It's a consciousness. It's a culture. It's what I've been brought up with. No matter what people say to me, 'you're not Black', 'you're this or you're that', as far as I'm concerned I've been brought up in a Black culture.

When I pointed out to him that his father was white, he stated:

Yeah I have a white father, but it's strange really, I have a white father who's married a Black woman, who's always associated himself with Black people in terms of his friends, the place where he lives, he still lives within the Black community. His best friends and people he socialises with now are Black people.

I then asked him whether he regarded his white father as having adopted a Black culture, and he stated:

Well to a large extent yeah, to a large extent. Subconsciously though, for him he's very much of the mind you know 'it's regardless of your colour', people are people. He's always lived his life that way. For me, I've tried to sit and explain to him, he can't imagine or understand that I've experienced racism.

'Black' then is more than just a colour. It has greater significance for Adrian in the sense of it representing a way of life within his social environment. For him, 'Black' is a consciousness and rides above the superficiality of skin-tone. He thinks 'Black' and acts 'Black' because he was raised in an extended family situation that saw him as a child mixing predominantly with his Black mother's side of the family.

David Jay, a man in his late twenties, also defined himself as 'Black British' and found the term 'half-caste' offensive. When I put it to him that he had a white mother and, as such, how did he then reconcile the fact that he 'excluded' her in his definition of his 'racial self', he stated:

That's just the way it is, since I was growing up in the family, in school, college and so on, I've been seen as a Black person, and that's how I've identified myself and that's how people have identified me . . .

Again, as with Terry and Adrian, to a large extent David's view of himself is wrapped up in the reality of his social existence. This reality is that he lives in a 'white society' in which he is viewed as Black regardless of how 'racially mixed' he is. In this way theories of 'mixed racial identity' (see Chapter 1) have little or no relevance if they are not connected to the social reality of lived and *subjective* experience.

Marlon Hasson, in his early thirties, viewed himself as 'Black British' and also found the term 'half-caste' demeaning and abhorrent. In regard to articulating his 'racial self' he pointed out:

> I am Black and I am British. I am Black and I am British and I do not seek to deny that. Different people would like me to deny that and say well you are not Black you are British. However, the system does not allow you to work that way.

In terms of Marlon conceptualizing his mixed origin identity, within his definition of himself, he stated:

> my dad is African, he's Somali, he's African, I am of a different colour to what the majority of the race is here [in Britain]. They let me know that I am different. I feel different in many many respects, not just because of my colour, but because of the ways of thinking, of doing things, the way we have to depend on each other and so forth. You know, I don't deny the white side of me, of my family, of my blood, I don't deny that at all. However, the way that I've lived in the last 34 years makes me feel I am more wanted or loved and embraced being Black and with Black people.

As with the other 'younger men' respondents, Marlon relates to how the broader community impacts on one's conception of 'self' in the racialised sense. Much of his definition rests on the notion of 'belonging'. It is clear that he feels by and large excluded from the broader 'white society', regardless of his mother being white and part and parcel of the 'white community'. Marlon sees his 'place' in the context of the city of Liverpool as being inextricably interwoven with that of his father's. To paraphrase Parmar, Marlon's father is the post-colonial migrant who inhabits a history of diaspora and Marlon is his mixed origin offspring.[6] Hence, they are linked not only in 'blood' but in the 'otherness' of social identity within the context of the British Empire and its colonial past.

Terry Woan, a man in his mid-twenties, found the term 'half-caste' offensive and would never associate himself with it. He, like all of the other younger men, prefered the term 'Black British'. However, Terry qualified his definition with further insight and food for sociological thought:

> I say I'm Black British but I don't feel like a Briton. You know in terms of how you'd think of the British Empire or the British people. I say that I'm Black but I feel a little uncomfortable saying that cos I am of mixed race. Obviously there's two sides within me and certain, for want of a better word, 'full' Blacks may not think that or see me as Black. I've always thought that in the past . . . Ultimately I see myself as Black British. But it's not a perfect way of saying what I am.

There is a sense of 'Black community spirit' in the definitions of the 'racial self' put forward by the younger men. Terry encapsulates the very complex nature of trying to define yourself as a person of mixed origin descent in British society in the 1990s. He saw himself as 'Black British' yet he also stated that 'it's not a perfect way of saying what I am'. Who would disagree with him? Indeed, and in line with the work of the sociologist Stuart Hall,[7] in stating what it is to be 'Black' in the 1990s there can never be a straightforward definition which covers the whole spectrum of a person's existence.

Nevertheless, it is evident in interpreting the younger men's responses to the question of their 'racial self' that it has been shaped to a large degree by the social forces around them. The 'colossal weight' of questioning their identities is part of what makes it an unenviable task balancing white and Black parentage in a society that undermines one side of the parental line (Black), while elevating the other (white). Without exception, all the younger men felt that it was taken for granted within their life experience to define themselves as being 'Black British'. This is the definition which, although far from perfect, makes the more sense in relation to their social condition and environmental surroundings.

c) The older women (born between 1925 and 1945)

Turning now to the older women, 67-year-old Ada Hall described herself as 'Black British' *now*. However, she recognised that when she was younger she did not use the term 'Black British' to define herself. She implied, if in a somewhat tongue-in-cheek manner, that the definition of her 'racial self' was bound up in whatever was the latest term in vogue in the 'Black community'. As she pointed out: 'Well now we use Black don't we? But when I was younger we were coloured or "half-caste."' I then asked her why she no longer used the term 'half-caste' to describe herself and she replied in rhetorical fashion: 'Well they say it's wrong don't they? No one's a caste are they? Nobody's half of something are they?'

Interestingly, in the first interview with Ada she stated that she did not find the term 'half-caste' offensive. Yet in the second interview extract she implicitly suggested and was prepared not to use the term in defining herself because 'the Black community says so'. There did not seem to be any conviction in her understanding of the negative connotations attached to the term 'half-caste'. For Ada, it was simply that 'we don't use it anymore, so I won't'.

Unlike Ada, Emma Okuru, in her early sixties, found the term 'half-caste' offensive and did not associate herself with it. She simply defined herself as 'Black', thus excluding her mother from her definition of her 'racial self', and disregarding the fact that she was of mixed origin descent. She replied:

> Well you see whatever I think of my mother is private, but I am seen as a Black woman by whites and that is even if some Blacks don't accept me.

Emma raised, *inter alia*, the issue of 'Black acceptance' in regard to her 'racial self'. She said that some will not accept her as 'Black' even though whites will view her as such. It appears to be a dilemma faced by a number of the respondents too, both young and old in this study: the issue of 'Black acceptance'. Yet regardless of the possibility of not being 'accepted' by some 'full-Blacks', Emma was adamant about her own 'racial self' being defined as 'Black'.

The issue of 'Black acceptance' is a theme which would require further research and the questioning of 'full-Blacks' within the city of Liverpool context. Due to the usual time constraints involved in qualitative studies, the scope of the present research could not deal specifically with this theme at an in-depth level. However, Chapter 3 (below) provides useful insights, as it examines the social interaction of the respondents within the Black community of Liverpool.

Doreen Kray, who was 62 years of age at the time of the interviews, found the term 'half-caste' meaningless; nevertheless she admitted that it had deep significance within the Liverpool Black experience. In recalling how her family dealt with the term 'half-caste', she stated:

> we used to be called 'half-caste', and I remember, I'm sure it was part of the discussion in the family cos we were always talking about it, I remember somebody saying to me once that nobody's 'half' anything. And I know my parents didn't like the term . . . I think there was a preference for using the term 'coloured', which seemed a lot better.

When I asked her to elaborate on the reason why 'half-caste' was such a bad term to use she replied:

> I think that it didn't make sense and the fact that someone said to me that nobody's 'half' of anything made sense to me. It's like the old term of talking about your 'better half' in your marriage, you know if you start talking about marriage in those terms it's usually the woman who's the other 'half', the man is rarely the 'half', he's the 'whole' person and she's the 'half'. You know it never made any sense [she laughs]. So I didn't like it. Don't forget I was growing up [as an adult and politically] in the 1960s when the American thing was developing [Civil Rights Movement, 'Black is Beautiful', etc.]. And the influence then of Black music [was strong].

Doreen has continued her journey of defining herself to the extent that she is now more comfortable with the term 'British-born African'. She says that it was a long journey of self-discovery and contemplation before she arrived at this definition of her 'racial self'. She explains it this way:

It has been a gradual change, I now define myself as a 'British-born African'. . . . In terms of race and ethnicity, I mean it needed a cultural dimension, which being 'Black' didn't explain what the relationship was to that African background. And the more I read about African tradition, the more I wanted to recognise that background.

It is apparent that Doreen has thought deeply about her racial origins and related her discovery of the 'racial self' to 'a gradual change'. The importance of 'knowing thy self' is also something which emerges from my interviews with Doreen (I had two in-depth interviews with her lasting up to 3–4 hours). Indeed she had not come to define herself as being 'British-born African' overnight; it had been a long process for her. No doubt her inner reflection of the 'racial self' was conditioned by her life experience and being involved in 'Black community' issues over the previous thirty years. It should be pointed out that she was a respondent who 'does have something to say' about her racial origin which may well be beyond the scope of the 'average' respondent in this study. Nevertheless the contribution is more than relevant as she fits the criteria for this study just as well as the other respondents.

Mary Ikem, in her late fifties, was less philosophical about how she saw herself. She also found the term 'half-caste' derogatory and refused to use it. When I asked her how she defined herself as a person she stated: 'I am just Black and I just look at myself as being a Black woman.'

I asked her to elaborate as to why she had come to this definition of being a 'Black woman'. She replied:

Let's see, when I was younger . . . you know when you are young you're just going about your business. You know you're looking to enjoy yourself and things like that, but you see, sometimes you say your colour doesn't matter, you like me for who I am. But having got older and having had children your colour does matter and you are Black. And the thing is wherever you go the first thing people see is you're Black and then you're a woman or a man after that. You know there's no getting away from that. And neither do I want to get away from it. I've got nothing to be, I don't have to explain my Blackness to anyone – that's it.

With Mary, as with Doreen, there is a development in her racial consciousness which has led to her definition of being a 'Black woman'. Her life experience of living in societies such as the UK and US has determined to a large extent her understanding of 'who she is' in a racial sense. It is her skin-tone which is the 'first thing they see' that determines what she is in the world; it is secondary to her being a woman. However, 'Blackness' was not a burden for Mary, she was proud of it and 'does not have to explain it to anyone'.

Jean Stevens, in her early sixties, gave a 'raceless' definition of herself. She didn't take to terms such as 'half-caste' when she was young and said 'she didn't know what they were talking about'. In relation to how she saw herself she stated:

> I'd define myself as a person first . . . I'd just define myself as an ordinary human being that has grown up to be not what I was expected to be probably . . . personality wise, I've not been a person to feel that I'm different from anybody else. And I feel I am what I am. I couldn't be any different. I make mistakes like everybody else . . . I'm just a grandmother and a mother. I help people and, erm, I'm just an ordinary person I think.

Jean had a very individualist approach to her definition of her 'racial self'. It was not bound to what the 'Black community' or 'white community' prescribed. Rather it was more in line with her own defiance of her right to be a human being, and to be treated as such was for her the most important thing. She did not like labels which place a human being in a particular 'racial pigeon-hole'. She was 'just an ordinary person'. However, considering the entire interview, she did point out the reality of her African husband not being able to find a job as a medical doctor in Liverpool when they were courting in the late 1940s. Also, she recalled how her father could not fulfil his dream to be a schoolteacher in England due primarily to his distinctly African/Brazilian racial origins. So she had experienced racism in her life but refused, it seems, to let it rule her own understanding of what it is to be human. In the collective lives of the older women in this study we can see both the impact of individual thought and the broader community in helping to shape their definitions of the 'racial self'. Let us now consider the views of the younger women.

d) The younger women (born between 1960 and 1975)

Anita Craven was in her twenties and from the younger generation, and described herself as 'Black British', but this definition
did not come easily to her. She did not ever use the term 'half-
caste' to define herself and found it a demeaning and degrading
phrase. When I asked her to explain further her feelings of coming
to such a definition of herself as 'Black British', knowing that
she also had a white mother, she replied:

> Like I've said, when I was younger it was a need to have an
> identity, a lot of us of mixed race didn't have an identity.
> Your mum was white and your dad was Black, a lot of us
> were brought up by our mothers who were white. So where
> is your identity? We all thought Black was being a colour.
> And because we were all so fair [in colour] we could have
> pushed for 'white'. As the word 'Black' was derogatory then
> wasn't it? But now because the word 'Black' is positive it's
> different. I feel personally before that I didn't have an iden-
> tity, it was like crushing the lid on where it was. Obviously
> I'm not bitter about my mum being a white mother, because
> I think a lot of my strength comes from her. But at the end
> of the day, for my own personal identity, I need to say that
> I'm a Black woman. That's where I'm focused from and that's
> where I'm coming from.

It appeared to me that Anita viewed 'Black' as being more
than just a colour, so I asked her to explain what she thought
it was. She said:

> Oh yes, it's far more than a colour [Black] . . . I think that it's
> your roots, it's your identity, and it's not about the colour
> Black, but what's inside your soul, as far as I'm concerned.
> Wanting to know where I belong, and that is my own cul-
> ture. Because where is our culture, our culture is Africa, but
> we don't live there, we live in Liverpool. So you have to have
> some identity, and that is my own personal identity, of what
> I belong to.

Time and again that 'sense of belonging' is raised by the respondents. The ambiguity of the 'racial self' being of mixed origin
is something which I found was dealt with in a rather logical

manner by Anita. She felt no bitterness toward her white mother. Indeed she acknowledged openly that she gained much of her inner strength from her. Yet she also had an understanding of the 'outside world' and how that separates her from her mother in a manner that needs to be explained, theoretically and from a historical perspective (see Chapter 1). In other words, Anita on the micro level of her understanding of the 'racial self', can identify with her white mother emotionally, in terms of love, compassion and so forth, but on the macro level of society she also realises that she must have an identity that secures her own psychological well-being. This she found through defining herself as a 'Black woman' and/or 'Black British'. This is not a rejection of her mother, merely a realisation of her own 'racial self' within the *broader* society.

Diane Armstrong was in her early thirties and was arguably the respondent who most detested the term 'half-caste': she described herself as 'African/Black' in our first interview. But in the second interview, when asked again, she stated:

> I define myself as a Black woman in a political sense. Don't get me wrong, I know I don't get involved enough on Black women's groups and things like that, but that's because of time really. I still feel that I know enough. There's still a hell of a lot more I've got to learn as well. That's probably something I'd like to do in the future, get involved in Black women's committee's and whatever.

I asked Diane to explain further what she actually meant by viewing herself as a 'Black woman' and why it appeared so important to her. She stated:

> I am Black in the fact that I want Black children, I eat Black food, I listen to Black music, I still move in a Black circle. Although I work with a lot of white people and go to meetings where I'm the only Black person, I still move in my personal life in a Black circle. As in with my friends, do you know what I mean? I have got white friends as well, but they also move in Black circles as well. They live with Black men and have got Black children. I'm an open person whereas I can get on with anybody, I don't let the fact that I'm Black stop me going to white areas and stop me working, I switch on and off. Being a Black woman is a way of life. And I want

to put all my energies into the Black community in terms of being a role model for young Black women.

There was a definite sense of responsibility to the 'Black community' which Diane felt compelled to live up to. She recognised the fact that she had to move between 'Black' and 'white' in her work and social life. Yet she appeared to feel no stress in interacting with these worlds. The renowned African American scholar W. E. B. Du Bois described this behavioural trait as a form of 'double consciousness'[8] – living as a Black person and interacting in a predominantly 'white world'. Diane's food, music and social life were 'Black', this was important to her. It did not prevent her from mixing with 'white' people, and it did not make her bitter or withdrawn from society. She simply recognised the way she wanted to live on a personal level and endeavoured to marry this with her everyday social interaction with the 'white world'. Diane came to accept that racism is an everyday reality in British society. This is particularly borne out in the fact that she wanted to be a 'role model for young Black women' in the Black community. Therefore her sense of the 'racial self' was bound up with an understanding of the broader struggle Black people face against institutionalised racism/sexism in society. It goes beyond a personal definition as it is infused with a sense of responsibility for her social group and broader community.

Jean Williams was in her late twenties and, like both Anita and Diane, found the term 'half-caste' highly offensive and refused to use it as 'racial label'. She preferred the terms 'Liverpool-born Black' or 'Black British', if pushed. However, Jean clearly did not take to the idea of 'labelling' a person in any sense. As she stated:

> I'm just a Black woman. You know, a Black woman. I'm aware of the hassles of being Black, I'm aware of hassles being a woman, I'm aware of hassles being a single mother! You know it's like I'm continuously getting labels put on to me and having to try and justify and prove that I'm not part of that stereotype. You know people continuously label you.

When I asked her how she came to terms with the added complexity of being of mixed racial origin and having a white mother, yet still defined herself as a 'Black woman', she replied:

I don't like when you start splitting and dividing into squares. I really object to it, because when the crunch comes to crunch I'm always called 'Black this or Black that' so why when it suits them to 'split' me into parts should I go along with it? No, I don't like it, I am a Black woman, that's it really. Black is a term for me, it's not me shade, cos we come in all shades, whatever, it's about me, my own culture and my ancestors. It's no point saying I've got a white mum and a Black dad, this doesn't carry with nobody when they see me in the street as a Black woman. At the end of the day I'm a Black woman, that's what I am, it's what I am.

Even though Jean disliked the everyday identification labels society puts on persons/groups, like most people who are asked to give a description of what defines them, she still ended up labelling herself a 'Black woman'. Indeed, can labelling ever be avoided in modern societies such as the UK? It is very doubtful whether it is actually possible *not* to label social groups in society. At least not until there is the utopia of social equality, and opportunity that is fairly distributed in society in terms of 'race', class, gender and so forth. In this sense, the respondents are under the same pressure as anyone else, even if they refuse 'to play the game', to describe their 'ethnic origin/s' if asked.

Jill Harlem was a young respondent in her mid-twenties who defined herself in a number of ways: sometimes as 'mixed race', but ultimately she saw herself as a 'Black woman'. She stated:

I see myself as mixed race, on application forms I'm either 'Black UK', 'Liverpool-born Black', or of African descent, depending on which application forms I'm filling in. But I'm always conscious of the fact that I offend me dad when I say I'm Black. Cos, as I say, he says that it denies the whiteness [in her].

Although Jill was sensitive to her father's feelings, during the interview she did point out that she would never have 'light-skinned' children on account of the possibility that they would encounter 'identity confusion'. I therefore asked her how she reconciled this with knowing that she had a white father. She replied:

he wouldn't take offence because it would be my decision. I've tried to explain to him that, regardless of him, when people see me walking down the street they see me as a Black woman. So I'm not seen as a 'white girl', I'm seen as a 'Black girl'. And he's aware of the fact that I'm strong on my convictions of being a Black person.

A strong theme emerging from the respondents is the realisation that whatever they may think of themselves on a personal level (and also what their parents think), the broader 'white society' is more than likely to see them as 'Black' or other than white. Although this is particularly clear in terms of Jill's life experience, it also appears as a strong theme in both the older and younger generations.

The final young female respondent, Mary Franklin, was also in her mid-twenties and describes herself as a 'Black woman'. When I asked her to explain this definition in relation to the fact that she had a white mother, she pointed out:

> I like to think that I've got two constructs, one where I see myself as a Black woman, but I also recognise that I do have a white mother. And I am of mixed parentage. That is part of me, my whole physical and emotional make-up, that is me.

In many respects Mary provides a way of explaining the complexity of defining oneself as a person of mixed origin descent in a society which is highly 'race' conscious. She has 'two constructs' which contain her 'racial self', one recognising the 'Black woman' in regard to the social reality of her interaction with the 'outside' world, and the other giving her the *inner* definition of knowing that she is of 'mixed parentage'. The latter acts, possibly, as a psychological antidote in relation to the relationship she has with her white mother.

How the respondents define themselves in a racial sense is paramount in terms of this study. The individual responses given above have drawn out a number of themes which can be seen as having a *collective* correlation in both generations. Table 2.1 shows how the respondents define themselves.

Table 2.1 shows the majority of the respondents relating to the word 'Black' in some shape or form. Indeed 18 out of the 20 preferred to describe themselves as 'African/Black', 'Black

Table 2.1 How the respondents define themselves by racial origin

	Racial definition
Older men	
Ian Taylor	Black
Harry Fredricks	Black British and Liverpool-born Black
William Billing	Liverpool-born Black
Stan Staunton	'half-caste'
Chris Jones	'half-caste' and Black man
Younger men	
Terry Frost	Black British and Black man
Adrian Jefferies	Black British
David Jay	Black British
Marlon Hasson	Black British
Terry Woan	Black British
Older women	
Ada Hall	Black British and 'half-caste'
Emma Okuru	Black
Doreen Kray	British-born African
Mary Ikem	Black British
Jean Stevens	'A person'
Younger women	
Anita Craven	Black British
Diane Armstrong	African/Black
Jean Williams	Liverpool-born Black
Jill Harlem	'mixed race' and Black woman
Mary Franklin	Black woman and mixed origin

British', 'Black', 'Black man', 'Black woman' or 'Liverpool-born Black'. However, 5 of the respondents also used the terms 'half-caste', 'mixed race' or 'mixed origin' interchangeably with 'Black'. Neither did they see this as a contradiction, it simply made logical sense to them personally. Two of the respondents did not use the term 'Black' in their definitions. One preferred to describe herself as 'a person' and the other as a 'half-caste' – both these respondents were from the older generation.

In regard to the term 'half-caste', it was interesting to see whether or not there was a generational shift in the use of the term by respondents. Table 2.2 shows that out of the older generation 5 respondents found the term 'half-caste' offensive and 5 inoffensive. The entire younger generation found the term offensive. Whether this is an indication of a change in the

Table 2.2 How the respondents view the term 'half-caste'

	Offensive	Inoffensive
Older generation:	5	5
Younger generation:	10	
Total:		20

collective racial consciousness of persons of mixed origin descent in the city of Liverpool cannot be fully established, yet it may well reflect a transformation. In view of the in-depth interviews it would not be out of place to suggest that 'half-caste' as a term is far less favourable to the younger generation than it is to the older. In point of fact many of the respondents noted the link between the terms 'Liverpool-born Black' and 'half-caste'. As such it may be reasonable to argue that racial consciousness has transformed in the collective sense of the mixed origin population in the city of Liverpool.

Parental influence in the construction of a racialised identity

It would be wrong to underplay or deny the potential that the parent or guardian has in shaping the early years of a child. As the interviews were conducted with adult respondents, an aim was to find out which of their parents, if any, had the most significant influence in relation to the shaping of their individual characters and world-views. Again, as with the definition of the 'racial self', it was important to allow the respondents as far as it is possible to 'speak for themselves'.

a) The older men

When I asked Ian Taylor which of his parents had influenced him the most in terms of his character-building, he stated:

> Ah, very hard. My dad give me purpose to do the best at what ever you do. Always be honest with yourself, you've got to do things in life where some people will feel you shouldn't fit in, but that's you. My mam give me kindness, the compassionate part of me, so who influenced me? I think it was quite even if I look at it properly. They both gave me something.

Harry Fredricks gave this response to the same question:

> Well I'd say me mother simply because when my father died
> I was four. But I believe my mother carried on what my father
> believed ... she carried on my father's principles. It's what
> she believed in.

It is not surprising Harry would say that his mother was the
major influence on his character, as earlier he pointed out how
she had taught him his 'awareness of racism' and how not to
use the term 'half-caste'. Also, due to the death of his father,
she had to raise the family for a long time on her own in the
1930s. Understanding this era in hindsight, Harry's mother must
certainly have had a strong character to withstand the social
conditions of her time and still raise a 'Black' family. It was
clearly evident in the interview with Harry that he had a deep
respect for his mother and the way in which she had educated
him concerning racism in society.

William Billing found it difficult to pin-point which parent
had influenced him the most and for what reasons. He said:

> That's difficult, in terms of putting into us [himself and his
> siblings] respect, me dad was very strong, disciplined. The
> discipline was clear from me dad. Although me dad wasn't
> there all the time due to him being away at sea. But he was
> so powerful. He also influenced me, people say I'm a sort of
> er, I've got strong leadership qualities. Now I was the eldest ...
> my dad also used to say before he went away to sea, 'I'm
> putting you in charge to look after your mother while I'm
> away'. It gave me a lot of responsibility as a kid. I mean, in
> the African culture the eldest, the first born, is seen to be a
> leader. He's [his father] given me all that. I think me mother
> was er, I think later on I realised all what she's been through
> as a white woman and the way she always put us first. And
> actually sacrificed, although she wouldn't, if she was here now
> she wouldn't say she understood racism. But she protected
> us in the way she operated. Erm, always making sure, be-
> cause of the issues of racism, she always made sure that we
> were better than anybody else. That our clothes were clean
> and nobody could criticise us. And she did that sort of thing
> in her own way, and in looking back I think that was important.

We never had much money, but she did her best to make sure that we were clean.

William clearly acknowledges the influence of both of his parents. His father gave him the 'leadership qualities' and his mother gave him protection, as best she could, from the outside world. He also has respect for the way in which she had to cope with abuse from the white community for having married an African seaman. These aspects of his parents' lives are embedded firmly within his mind and have helped shape his character. Given the fact that William has achieved tremendous personal success in his career in the city of Liverpool, it may well be that he gained his inner strength to succeed primarily due to his parents' influence on his character.

Stan Staunton, in responding to the question, replied:

Well you couldn't say it was me father cos he wasn't round long enough you see [he died when Stan was a child]. He had the right ideas my father. He wanted to put us into music, he bought me a harp, I used to play the harp when I was little. And he made sure that we were reared on some music. Which is good isn't it? He wanted us to learn music cos he was a good guitar player and wanted us to follow in his footsteps. You know which is good. Yeah it was good, but he wasn't around long enough.

When I asked whether his mother had influenced him in any manner Stan pointed out:

Not in music, she wasn't interested. But she was a very hard working woman who took care of us the best she could. I suppose I learned to work hard from her, along with me father, but he wasn't here long enough you see. My mam had to bring us up virtually on her own. She worked hard you know, it was hard times in them days.

Again, as with the other older male respondents, Stan gave credit to both his parents in a complementary fashion. His father gave him the inspiration to be a musician and taught him how to love it as an art. His mother gave him the 'work ethic' and the character to fight on in times of adversity. There is a respect for both his parents which comes through in his response to the question.

Chris Jones was very terse in his reply:

> Well I think it was me father really cos he taught me to play the guitar. He taught a lot of Black lads in Liverpool. He was a great influence for a lot of others not only me.

However, Chris had earlier pointed out that his mother was very disciplined and made sure that he did his chores about the house. I was also very impressed with the way Chris was dressed as a child. During our interview he showed me many photographs from his childhood and it was clear that his mother had taken the time to make sure he was well clothed. This is important to point out in order to get a general sense of the entire interview. In terms of my understanding, I do not think that the above response to the 'parental influence' question is a fair reflection of his thoughts. With hindsight, it would have been wise to ask Chris to elaborate more. Nevertheless, it can be interpreted that he was highly influenced by his father as Chris also was a keen semi-professional musician. Just like his father, he has spent a great many years singing/performing in social clubs in and around the city of Liverpool. Music was a very important part of his life, and this influence has come from his father.

b) The younger men

Terry Frost from the younger men tactfully confronted the question of which parent has influenced him most. He stated:

> I think both have influenced me along the way, me mum and me dad. There is no way I could say that one, er, was over the other, no way. The two of them have been really like a great influence to me.

When confronted with the same question, Adrian Jefferies replied:

> I put that into two categories, one is, socially it would be my father, for in the social aspect it's always been his strong point, and I've got some of those tendencies. I like to enjoy myself.

You know, within limits. I still see him regular from a socialising point of view. The other side is my mother, she's achieved her aspirations, she's fairly well-off, and worked really hard for that. She's given me the discipline, she set the stall out for all that. The one who's always been there as a reminder to take the right road. Whereas me dad would be a little too laid back on things really. My mother was the one who had *more* influence and still does today. I would be wary of doing anything wrong, not that I couldn't handle it or anything. I just wouldn't want to upset her.

It is important to point out that Adrian's mother is a Black woman and his father is white. This was not, as Adrian himself remarked, a 'usual' 'Black/white relationship in the city of Liverpool context.[9] Also, Adrian's mother provided the 'discipline' and fortitude to 'do the right thing' in life, to stay on the 'right road'. His father provided the 'social side', the relaxation in life. Interestingly, this scenario does not fit with conventional stereotyping, which often portrays the Black woman as lacking in discipline and so forth. Yet Adrian's mother provided the example of how to get on in life by sheer hard work and determination.

It was clear that David Jay had a very strong 'Black' orientated way of life in terms of his friends at school, college and in later life. As such, it was interesting to have his views relating to which parent had most influenced him. He stated:

I think it was more me mother . . . I think it's because she tried to wake us up early about racism. Because if something went wrong I went to my mother. She'd say stand up for yourself and have a go . . . I suppose it was because my mother experienced it [racism] with my father and did all she could to fight it. She was forced to become aware of racism and help her family survive. I know that she got pressure [trouble from her family] for going with my father . . . she was from the North End [of Liverpool] so she was sort of ostracised from her side of the family. Then she came to live in Liverpool 8. Geographically those barriers are still there. But within the family over the years my mum has made contact with her family again.

For David, his mother represented the person who he could most articulate his experience of racism to. Although she was white, she understood what it is like to feel ostracised. Through her experience with her own family snubbing her for marrying David's father, she was able to find the strength to fight racism in order to protect her children. David did not see his mother as 'white', he saw her as his mother, the person with whom he was most able to discuss 'racial issues' in the context of experiencing racism in the city of Liverpool.

Marlon Hasson was more philosophical in his response to the question of parental influence. He stated:

> My dad, I think he influenced me the most, I think a lot of sons attach themselves to their dads, they want to be like them. Erm, my dad was a very peaceful man, he always wanted to work, never had a bad word to say about anybody. If you were to curse someone out in front of him, he wouldn't allow you to do that. No, he'd tell you to shut up and go and keep it to yourself. That is a lot to do with him being a Muslim. It's a lot to do with Islam. It's a peaceful religion. And many things, I look at my dad and I liked a lot of things that he did, always working, peaceful and being loved by everybody. Because he was a solidly genuine man. We would sit on occasions many years back and we'd talk about different sports people. He'd tell me about the folks back home. They were history lessons he was giving me at that time. Unfortunately he died a few weeks ago. I think when we sat and talked that they were history lessons. I remember having to go to assembly, church in school and not taking one bit of notice because it was all centred around white people. It was as if no Black people ever existed, no Black people ever fought in the war, you know in many many respects it came through my dad [his awareness].

Whether or not Marlon was overtly sentimental about his father due to his recent death is open to question. Nevertheless there is much in Marlon's statement to suggest that his father had been a major influence on him. His father was 'hardworking and peaceful' and this was a major influence on Marlon's perception of him. Also, during the interview Marlon gave a strong impression of his 'racial consciousness'. He was very politically aware of racial discrimination and he put this awareness down to his father's influence. He made no reference to his mother in terms of her having any influence on his character. Did he resent her for being white? This could be a reason for him not wanting to talk in-depth about her during our interview.

Terry Woan, like Marlon, was very aware of his father's African roots and history. He came across as a thoughtful and caring person who was devoted to a life as a single parent due to the untimely death of his Black female partner. When asked which parent had influenced him most, after a long pause, he stated:

> I think it was me mother ... Cos I had the most contact with her. She was the most caring side of the parents. Discipline was me father's side of the influence.

Terry did give the impression during the interview that his father was somewhat 'distant' from the family. It was his mother who did most of the looking after the children while his father worked. He saw his father as having provided the 'discipline' and his mother the 'caring' side of parental influence.

Yet this is not uniform with all the male respondents. Often it was the mother who provided the 'discipline' and fortitude to withstand adversity in life. The interviews certainly give much insight into the ways in which the mixed origin respondents managed to deal with the complexity of essentially living as 'Black', yet having a parent who was white (in colour). For example, a number of the white mothers were often robustly preparing and educating their children for a racial*ised* society in which their offspring would have to fend for themselves. Without the subjective insight of the respondents much would be left to conjecture regarding themes such as 'parental influence'. Taking into account the views of the male respondents, it was interesting to see how 'parental influence' cannot be simply pigeon-holed into 'tidy' boxes. We will now consider the female respondents' views relating to the theme of 'parental influence'.

c) The older women

Ada Hall explained to me that her father died when she was only 5 years of age. Therefore it was her mother who had the major influence on her life. Ada said 'she was a wonderful mother'.

Regardless of the 'hard times' of the 1930s her mother did a remarkable job bringing up her family, and Ada acknowledged this fact.

When I asked Emma Okuru which of her parents had most influence on her character, she pointed out:

> Me dad, he was a 'Bible puncher'... he talked to me, he told me tales, he told me Anansi stories [West African tales], about the spider. And about duppy. He was a ghost. And he'd tell me about the slave trade... but I just saw it as a story. He told me about South America and about how the Portuguese and Spanish wiped out the native population there. And he told me not to go to South Africa when I got older. He said cos blood will run red. And he said before the end of my life their will be a push for independence in South Africa...

When I asked Emma whether her mother had any influence in life she replied, 'no, only my father'. It was clear through the interview that Emma's feelings were particularly strong for her father. She never mentioned her mother much during the interview; when she did it was only in a cursory manner.

Doreen Kray had a more balanced approach to the question of which parent had the greater influence over her. She replied:

> Both in different ways, I think my mother in a strange way had very traditional rules of a woman's role, strangely enough. Although she was a working housewife most of her life, she went to work and that positively influenced me. She thought the way through life for me was to marry and have kids. And I think she never ever came to understand why I never married and had children. Well I couldn't have children so that solved that problem, but she still didn't understand why I didn't do what she saw as the normal way of doing things. So every boy I brought home ended up being a possible son-in-law, so she'd woo all these young men and be lovely to them and say when are you going to marry them [she laughs]. I stopped taking boyfriends home in the end cos I got fed up with my mother palming me off to every man, some of whom I was just friends with you know. In one way she positively influenced me cos she was very strong. Very determined and stubborn. I inherited that stubbornness, and arguing these

issues through with her helped me clarify my position. So that in a way may have been a negative way, but it was healthy to me. It helped me also deal with people outside who were equally traditional as her. My father was positive in the sense that he believed education was the thing. Education was your survival, your passport. He was very proud of me, he encouraged me to go to meetings. He positively encouraged my educational development and also to be self-sufficient. In many ways they both influenced me.

For Doreen, it was the collective influence of both her parents which she acknowledges gave her 'stubbornness' and 'determination' to succeed in life. Her mother was hard-working and wanted Doreen to 'settle down' and raise a family, while her father encouraged her to achieve an education and 'self-sufficiency'. In many ways Doreen's parents had strong 'middle-class' values which they passed on to her. Even though her childhood years were beset with the Great Depression and war, from the two interviews I had with Doreen, I was struck by the way in which she described the household and how her mother and father managed their lives in a very organised fashion. Taking into account that in 1933 Doreen's mother, in her late teens, was a single parent, it is a remarkable 'recovery' to have gone on to have had a stable family like the one described by her daughter. Having spent nearly four hours with Doreen during our two interviews, being shown family photographs, letters and so forth, I am convinced of the authenticity of her 'middle-class' orientated family background. It is all the more remarkable, as this 'Black' family was embedded within the broader social environment of poverty and racism in the city of Liverpool.

Mary Ikem lost her mother when she was 18 years of age. When I asked her which of her parents had influenced her most during her life she pointed out:

> I was very close to me dad . . . even when I was younger I always seemed to be close to me dad. I don't know why . . . he never hit me, he never hit me. He used to talk to me, lecture me, I used to think he was going to make me a nun [she laughs]. He never hit me, now me mother would give you a go along [spanking], no messing. But she'd forget about it straight away, she'd hit you and forget about it. But me

dad never ever hit me, but he'd sit and talk to me, you know sometimes you'd be saying in your mind 'shut up' [laugh], because he was lecturing me kind of thing. But I used to love it cos he'd tell me the tales of Africa. Now me mum would talk to ya, but not as much as me dad. Me dad would sit for hours, you know like me mum would go out to her sister's . . . well I'd be sitting there and me dad's sitting there and he'd make like African soup, you know for our suppa and all of that. . . . Oh yeah, me dad would have meetings in the house with his African friends [the Calibars], and they'd have the meeting and they'd all be talking African. You know laying the law down and this and that. And I was always around and I'd be listening. Although he never taught me to speak African, which I regret, I'd pick words up and they'd tell me what they mean. *And I always regret not learning the language fully.*

With Mary there is the strong influence from her father which emerges in her response. She does acknowledge her mother in terms of her being rather disciplinarian in nature. However, it was her father who was always 'lecturing' to her morally and telling her stories. Mary regretted not having been taught her dad's native African language. She recalled the meetings of her father's African friends and how they spoke their African tongue. Mary admitted having 'picked up' a few African words, but she never grasped the language fully. Yet regardless of not having learnt to speak her father's African language, she did pick up African food recipes, such as soup, which she still uses today.

In her response to 'parental influence' on her, Jean Stevens stated:

I definitely know that it was my father. Because he was very philosophical and, erm, I'd say he was a great influence on me really. He helped in the community too, working with people, he helped us a lot to do something with our lives . . . I take from both cultures, Black and white, and the good thing about his culture which was erm, respecting other people and the old people. I think the mixture of the cultures goes nicely together if you can mix it and see other people and their cultures give them a different angle. And our culture goes nicely together if you can mix it. I think us being of mixed race have a different culture again, we've developed our own culture.

Jean, like Mary, stated that it was her father who most influenced her character. She was inspired by his commitment to helping 'in the community' and his 'working with people'. Her father was also 'very philosophical'. Yet she also readily admitted that she took from both cultures, 'Black and white', in her lifestyle. She also stated that 'mixed race' people *per se* develop a culture that is somewhat unique from both those of Black and white. This is a very interesting statement as she inadvertently agreed with the notion of distinct 'races' and that persons of mixed origin descent become 'distinct' themselves from the 'races' which created them. Is this why Jean refused to describe herself as anything more than 'a person' (see Table 2.1)? It may well be that because she saw herself as 'neither Black nor white', she preferred to be regarded just as a 'human being', rather than being totally 'separated' from her parents' 'cultures'. This is of course mere conjecture as, taking the entire interview into account, it was evident that Jean had lived her life as a 'Black person', particularly with her partner being of African descent. Much of her cultural values and political awareness were also 'Black orientated'. Nevertheless, there still lingers a degree of doubt as to 'who and what' she believed she was as a person of mixed origin descent.

d) The younger women

Anita Craven was brought up solely by her white mother. Nevertheless I asked her how she was influenced by her mother in terms of Black culture. Anita put it this way:

> No I think none at all [being presented with Black culture], I think everyone was the same, your mum didn't tell you about being Black, you were a coloured girl [she laughs]. Or we knew we were 'half-caste' kids, but we never got told. And I think with white people you were caught in that trap, that's what you were called.

In regard to the term 'half-caste', I asked Anita whether her mother used it and she replied:

Probably, I think so yes. I think what it was then was if your mum was Black and your dad was Black then you were Black, but if your mum was white and your dad was Black you were 'coloured' or 'half-caste'. But all of a sudden the 'half-caste' thing was no longer to be said any more. It was derogative and you couldn't be called 'half-caste' any more. But we were definitely influenced by our mum.

There has certainly been a change in Anita's racial consciousness and awareness as she has grown from being a child, being looked after by a single-parent white mother, and into an independent young woman. She now regarded herself as a 'Black woman', but it had been a 'journey of discovery' for her. It was not something she had inherited from her mother's influence, it is something which had been consciously built up via her life experience of growing up in Liverpool, working in London, then returning to Liverpool, where she worked for a 'Black women's group' in relation to media studies. Crucially, Anita's 'Black'-orientated racial consciousness was formed primarily by *external* social factors beyond the confines of the family setting and her mother's influence.

When asked which parent had had the strongest influence on her Diane Armstrong replied:

Mainly me dad, only because me dad spent more time with us, as me mother was out working and me dad worked nights you see. So when we used to come home from school he used to take us out to cricket matches and things like that. We'd spend all weekend with me dad. He's always encouraged us and as I've said when we got a little bit older we started asking questions. He started to tell us about his life in Trinidad and what he had to do to get out the country. Cos we used to ask him why he left that lovely country and come here. And now that I've actually been there and seen where he's lived, met all his family and everything, I can understand. He couldn't get work over there. He seen the opportunity to get out the country and took it.

Diane clearly leant toward the influence of her father on her character. Indeed, as she herself turned out to be a singer, the musical influence is evident. She has also taken a keen interest in her father's roots and native background in Trinidad. This shows another aspect of her interest as an adult to locate herself within Black culture and to find out more about her own roots. Understanding her father's past experience was very important for Diane, and this came out during the interview session in which she talked at length about his arrival in England.

As Jean Williams was for the best part of her young life an orphan she could not state which 'parent' had influenced her most. However, she did point out that the family of her son's father was very supportive and influential on her. Jean explained that they were Nigerians. She also pointed out her own initiative for learning, and her thirst for knowledge was apparent: 'Getting factual information and sitting in a chair and studying, that's been a major resource.'

Jill Harlem stated that her mother is 'without a doubt' the major influence on her:

> she's always been the role model. And she's always been the one that I've looked up to. Because she's Black I'm sure that's where all my security came from. She relates, she knows, I'm not saying that our experiences have been the same, but at least at the end of the day . . . when I used to go home to me dad and said 'such and such a body's called me this' [a racialised name such as 'Nigger'], he'd say 'ok love'. He always used to say 'I can't understand it, but I'll do what I can for you'. Cos as a white man he could not understand the feelings I felt. But with me mum she would fully understand what I'd been through. My dad, actually, would be more aggressive and want to do something about it, but my mum would be well 'you know you've got to put up with this the rest of your life'.

In terms of racial consciousness and political awareness, Jill stated that her father tried harder than her mother to understand the issues:

> I think me dad over-compensates because of his whiteness to be that much more aware. More politically aware than me mum on the Black issues. But as much as he is politically aware, as much as he is radical, at the end of the day he is white and would never ever understand that first hand experience [of racism].

Again relating to her Black mother's influence Jill pointed out:

> She's always been the security. I don't know what it would
> be like to look up to a white mother; to run home from
> school to say such a body's called me a 'nigger' or something
> to a white mum. I think that's where my mum is security,
> because that Black role model was always there, always knew,
> always understood and always made it better.

Jill found comfort and security in her Black mother and stated
that her white father, although supportive, would not ever fully
understand the experience that she had of being a 'Black' woman
in British society. Her mother was her role model: 'without a
doubt'. Jane stated that she did not know what it would be like
to have a white mother to look up to. Yet if we take the example
of David Jay earlier, who was a very 'Black conscious' character,
his mother is white and was *the* parent who protected him against
the evil of racism. In addition, returning to the older generation, Harry Fredricks revealed how his white mother also provided
him with the strength to tackle racism. Therefore, although Jane
readily admitted, and many commentators would agree with her,
that her father as a white person would never fully understand
the experience of racism, it does not necessarily mean that white
mothers and fathers of Black children are incapable of providing both education and psychological *support* for their Black
children.

Mary Franklin confirms again how the white mother and the
Black father can each influence their mixed origin offspring, as
she stated:

> I think they've both had an equal input, erm I think my
> mum's had a great influence on me, but it's not because she
> happens to be the white parent. I think that she's got a powerful
> personality, and one that would influence anybody basically.
> Now you see me dad, he was very much there as we were
> growing up. So he was there at the most important stage I
> would say. You know, he used to do things like comb our
> hair and he was showing the other side of the culture [the
> Black, African Caribbean, culture], very much so, yeah.
> And that was very important. So they both influenced me
> really.

Table 2.3 Parental influence on the mixed origin respondents

Influence	No.
Equal from both parents:	9
Solely the mother:	5
Solely the father:	5
Neither parent:	1
Total:	20

There is in the experience of Mary Ikem the suggestion that 'influence' can move beyond the 'colour' of a parent. For Mary, it was her white mother's 'powerful personality' that influenced her own character building. Yet she still acknowledged her father's contribution and influence on her cultural awareness. Earlier it was pointed out how Mary had major problems as a child confronting white racism in the school setting, in terms of name-calling and so forth. This may have caused someone else to become bitter toward white people in general, but Mary displayed no bitterness in her comments. Neither did she feel in some way 'distant' from her white mother because she was 'white'. On the contrary, her mother's strong personality gave Mary the strength to overcome the adversity of the racial taunts she had and may continue to receive from the broader society. The point here is that even if the society in question is hostile and racist toward the mixed origin person, this does not necessarily manifest itself in the relationship between the white parent and the mixed origin offspring. The interviews corroborate that many of the white parents provided necessary support to the mixed origin child so that they may be able to combat the inevitable racial slurs that will beset them in life. Table 2.3 shows how the respondents viewed 'parental influence'.

Table 2.3 reveals a majority of 9 respondents stating that both parents had influenced their characters. Five said that it was their mother alone who had influenced them most. Interestingly, 2 of the 5 mothers were the only Black mothers in the study – being the parents of a younger male and female respectively. Five of the respondents stated that it was their father who had most influence over them. Finally, one respondent (Jean Williams, from the younger generation) had spent her early years mainly as an orphan and stated that she had no parental influence as such. However, she did point out that her Nigerian 'in-laws' had a strong impact on her social and cultural development.

Conclusion

The importance of understanding how the mixed origin respondents come to construct the 'racial self' and, in turn, how the 'parental influence' has impacted on them cannot be overstated. Indeed, this chapter reveals some important insights into how a mixed origin person born and raised in the city of Liverpool has come to terms with his or her complex social identity construct. In this sense, the subjective insights of respondents 'speaking for themselves' make a significant contribution to the theoretical works cited in Chapter 1, and to the 'old literature' particularly.[10] Indeed, the responses to the themes in the interviews reveal that the mixed origin respondents take a rather pragmatic approach. By and large the respondents appear to realise subjectively that they are of mixed racial heritage, but seem to comprehend the objective social reality of 'not being white' in British society. In addition, and referring to the 'old literature' on 'mixed race' persons, it would be wrong to suggest that collectively the mixed origin respondents display signs of 'psychological malaise'. It would be more appropriate to suggest that they deal with the complexity of being of mixed origin descent in a rather sensible and *knowing* manner. Indeed the majority and most racially conscious, 'Black orientated' respondents gave respect and acknowledgement to their respective white parent.

Another theme which emerges is connected to the 'racial self and the parent'. As acknowledged, the respondents had an understanding of themselves personally as 'not being white', therefore realising that they were 'different' from the parent who happened to be from the dominant white culture (in this case study, 18 were white women and 2 were white men). Yet this 'difference' did not necessarily mean that the mixed origin offspring would not find support from the white parent in terms of dealing with the effects of everyday racism. Rather it has been shown that some of the white mothers were very instrumental in educating their children (who are all now adults) about the racism they will face in 'white society'.

Even if the white parent did not 'educate' their mixed origin offspring about racism in society, it was revealed overwhelmingly that the respondents viewed their white parent as being somehow 'separate' from the broader 'white community'. Put another way, the 'whiteness' of the parent was largely insignificant to the respondent, and he/she viewed their parent as being part and parcel of a 'Black' family structure which inevitably had to deal with the 'outside world' in a *collective* sense. In short, the white parent becomes either 'colourless' or is regarded as 'Black' *orientated* within the family setting. The notion of a 'white parent' who is 'Black' orientated again is something not readily discussed in the 'old' or 'new' literature concerning mixed racial identity.

This chapter also reveals that the majority of the respondents see themselves as 'Black' (i.e. with variations such as 'Black woman', 'Black British' and 'Liverpool-born Black') in British society. This is particularly evident among the younger respondents in the study. It does indicate a change in the way persons of African mixed origin descent in Liverpool view themselves. There was a time when a term such as 'half-caste' was commonplace within the city of Liverpool context. Since the late 1960s this term has become increasingly despised and seen as derogatory by many persons within the Liverpool 'Black' community. The reason the term is seen as detestable is apparent in many of the responses given by the younger generation particularly. Admittedly some members of the older generation found the term 'half-caste' inoffensive, but this could be expected given the time and historical moment which shaped their life experiences in the 1930s. That is not to suggest that it was a 'clean-cut' split between the older and younger generations in terms of their racial consciousness. This was not so, for a number of the older generation, male and female, found the term 'half-caste' demeaning and would not use it to describe themselves. Therefore racial consciousness should not be seen as something static and measurable, but rather something which straddles generations. Usually there is never a 'complete break' from the past: it takes time before 'old' racial terms become obsolete.

Another theme which emerged from the respondents' comments relates to the issue of 'Black acceptance'. Emma Okuru suggested that, regardless of whether or not 'full-Blacks' accepted her, she viewed herself as being 'Black'. As with many of the other respondents, for Emma it was in the social reality of her existence which brought her to the self-definition of being 'Black'. She was not responsible for the thoughts of other Black people (or white) who would deny her the 'right to be Black'. The 'Black-on-Black' interaction theme will be covered further in Chapter 3.

Crucially, it is in how the respondents view themselves in relation to the broader society which reveals much about their collective racial awareness and consciousness. It is evident from many of the comments made by the respondents that they viewed their existence in British society as resting primarily on how they were seen by the 'outside world'. In addition, the majority had not fully grasped 'who they were' until they had reached the adult stage in their lives. Many did point out that they knew they were 'not white', but coming to terms with their 'racial self' was more complex than that for a person of African mixed origin descent. This point is corroborated by the current debate taking place in the US regarding 'multiracial identity' (see Chapter 1). Coming to terms with a 'multiracial heritage' presents a number of dilemmas for the person/s involved. Moreover, it can often be a 'colossal weight' making sense of the *diasporan* 'racial self' in the *post*modern world.[11] This chapter has covered two important themes relating to the development of a racialised identity among persons who could claim a 'multiracial heritage'. The following chapter will consider two more equally valid themes: 'Black-on-Black' social interaction and whether the respondents have ever considered changing their physical appearance.

3
Speaking for Themselves (II):
Inside and Outside of Blackness in Liverpool, UK

Half caste
Outcast
Miscast
Misused,
Confused . . .
Spirit . . .
Bruised.

Are we insane?

There's only ONE brain,
only ONE pain,
only ONE mind,
only ONE kind.

It's not a question of taste –
There's only **ONE** human race.
If we are to BE –
We must set Ourselves
FREE!

Tina Tamsho[1]

As with the previous, this chapter will examine two themes relating to the personal views of mixed racial origin respondents from Liverpool, UK. First, it will consider how they see themselves *within* the 'Black community' and how being of mixed origin descent impacts in terms of the 'light-skinned', 'dark-skinned' scenario. In other words, does skin colour/shade have relevance for the respondents? Moreover, is it of particularly significance to the Liverpool Black experience as it is for the African American? To gauge differences in the social construction of multiracial identity between the UK and US, via the respondents' views, should help to clarify a global understanding.

The second theme will consider the issue of whether or not the respondents have ever wanted to or thought about changing their physical appearance. In following this topic the aim is to gain a collective and broader insight as to the significance of 'racial self-hatred' and/or 'self-denial' among the multiracial respondents. For systematic purposes, as with the previous chapter, the structure of this chapter will cover the views of the 'older men', 'younger men', 'older women' and 'younger women' respectively.

Shades of Blackness

a) The older men

When asked whether the issue of skin colour/shade had any relevance in his experience in the Liverpool Black community, Ian Taylor stated: 'The older boys in the past [1950s] would conk their hair [straighten it from tight curly].'

He did not think that being light-skinned or dark-skinned had significance among the 'boys' when he was a young man. However, he did point out that 'it was really a girl thing, we had a few that thought they were white.' When prompted to explain this a little further he digressed and went on to talk about how the different generations of Blacks in Liverpool have changed from being in 'his day' a more unified group, to today, which is characterised by everyone fighting on individual platforms to be 'top jockey'. During the interview Ian implicitly suggested that the Black community is fragmented. Yet, according to Ian, the shade of one's skin had little to do with the disunity he perceived among the Black people in Liverpool. His position tended to focus on the impact of 'individualism' over 'collectivism' in regard to Black-on-Black interaction. It is this 'dog-eat-dog' mentality that presented the current impediment to Black unity – issues related to colour/shade for him are largely irrelevant.

Unlike Ian Taylor, Harry Fredricks felt one's 'shade of Black-ness' did have relevance to the Liverpool Black experience and he had much to say on the subject. As he pointed out:

> Oh it does, it certainly has relevance . . . You can find mixed race people looking on Black people as inferior you know. And it goes the other way too, some downgrade 'half-castes' you know in that derogatory manner. It just goes on and on really. People like to put themselves in little boxes. You will find that the African man will have a club, I mean it's not as much now, he doesn't have the amount of clubs now like in Liverpool, but they didn't want mixed race people in. They were the ones to be seen as mistrusted. Having said that, the given thing is that some of these Africans actually had mixed race children themselves. So this is a major contradiction you see. You know, people not thinking things through. If they just looked to themselves and say 'well I'm pulling mixed race people down and I've got mixed race children, something is wrong here'. Common sense would tell you that. But you see there is a helluva lot of racism amongst the Black race.

Harry was adamant about there being problems of racism among Black people in Liverpool. He continued:

> Racism is not only white inspired racism. It's not just simply Black versus white. It's a little more than that. You see there is always someone who has got to have someone as a whip-ping boy sort of thing [a scapegoat]. You can call him as a Black man, and you can call him as a China man, and you can call him as a Somali, and you can call him as an Arab, you know, and so on. But it's virtually the same racism, nothing changes. Racism is racism. And that's all there is to it. But you see the problem we have is that our people seem to think that it's only whites on Blacks.

Harry suggests strongly that there is a problem among Black people in Liverpool relating to one's particular racial origins. It is interesting how he earlier pointed out the contradictory be-haviour of some Africans who, on the one hand, rejected 'mixed race' persons, but on the other fathered them. Harry's views give some insight into Black-on-Black interaction; yet it is an area which needs further social investigation.

Indeed, William Billing also raised the issue of Black-on-Black social antagonism between the indigenous 'Liverpool-born Blacks' and the immigrant African Caribbeans in the 1970s. The irony here, as with Harry's views of Africans and 'Liverpool-born Blacks' in an earlier period, is that many of the African Caribbeans also had sons and daughters who would ordinarily be described as 'Liverpool-born Black'. What emerges from the views of Harry and William is the suggestion that there are three apparently distinct social groups of African descent which are, in many profound ways, interrelated within the Liverpool Black experience: Africans, African Caribbeans and 'Liverpool-born Blacks'.

Yet the complexity of Black-on-Black interaction does not end there, for we must also include the African American element. In point of fact many 'Liverpool-born Blacks' have or can trace an African American father. This is primarily due to the First and Second World Wars and the presence of an American military base in the north-west of England up to the 1980s. Many African American soldiers would come to the city of Liverpool on leave and make social contact with the Black community in night life entertainment. In point of fact, the eminent writer George Padmore in 1947 highlighted the 'problem of Negro GIs' children' in Liverpool after the Second World War.[2]

When asked for his views on Black-on-Black interaction and the issue of colour/shade, Stan Staunton replied:

> I've experienced something in that, because my hair wasn't curly. My mate used to call me a 'John Bull' [that's a local term for a 'white man' in Liverpool]. I said I can't help my hair the way it is can I. Makes no odds to me anyhow [he doesn't care] what your hair is like. I can't understand all that nonsense of lighter skin and that cos we're all Black aren't we? It's not our fault if some of us have lighter skin or straighter hair than others.

Interestingly, Stan saw no difference between Black people in Liverpool: 'we're all Black aren't we'? Yet earlier (see Chapter 2) when he was defining his 'racial self' he openly described himself as a 'half-caste' and further stated that he was 'half-Black', 'half-white'. Again, we could interpret his view that 'we are all Black' as a broader social reality of how Stan felt he was seen. Regardless of what he thought on a personal level, Stan suggested that whether you are 'light-skinned' or 'dark-skinned' you are still regarded as being Black. This theme emerges strongly among the multiracial respondents and has to be understood as a strategy for surviving psychologically in an incoherent human landscape where 'race' is a major social marker. Stan has a personal (micro) definition of himself and a broader societal (macro) view. If we fail to appreciate this aspect of his making sense of his world, then we fail to comprehend the complexity of his social existence. Crucially, Black-on-Black antagonism makes little sense to Stan as he saw both light-skinned and dark-skinned as one social group. However, he also acknowledged that friction does exist between socially defined Black groups in the city of Liverpool context; that is, in regard to phenotype characteristics such as hair texture and skin tone. Yet at bottom, for Stan it is all 'nonsense as we're all Black' and it is arguably *the* key factor in our social world.

Chris Jones did not experience any major problems within the Black community in terms of the colour/shade issue. This is probably due to him being in contact mainly with similar looking Blacks, in a phenotype sense, when he was growing up in Liverpool. He recalled:

> most of the lads I knocked around with were light-skinned . . . Sometimes people would say 'oh he's "quarter caste" or refer to the "half-caste boys" or "shine boys"', but there was never any real problem you know, they were just names at the end of the day.

For Chris, racial labels were 'just names at the end of the day'. There was no real problem with 'quarter caste', 'half-caste' and so on. He did not see the negative racial connotations behind such terms as many of the other Liverpool respondents did. Again this indicates how racial labelling affects persons in different ways. One's individual experience will to a large extent determine the outlook one has on the issue of racial categorisation. We will now consider the younger men's views on Black-on-Black social interaction.

b) The younger men

When Terry Frost was asked to give his thoughts on Black-on-Black social interaction in the city of Liverpool context he pointed out:

> Sometimes you can be too Caribbean for somebody, you can be too Caribbean for them. How I'm talking now like, when some people hear me talking people say well like 'how come Terry's talking like that?' All type of stupidity like that. But at the end of the day I feel no way [meaning he doesn't care] cos I have to fly the flag [be what I am].

Terry was asked to explain his thoughts on the colour/shade issue in the context of his experience in Liverpool, and he replied:

> Well you know we've got problems with people who don't like Africans, they don't really like Africans, you've got people out there who don't like people from the Caribbean. It's as if they can't identify with people who are coming from Africa or the Caribbean. It's like a heavy culture shock... It's a deep culture shock for some of the 'Liverpool-born Blacks' to cope with [smile].

Terry found it difficult to answer why it was that he thought some 'Liverpool-born Blacks' had problems with Africans and Caribbeans. Again his opinion brings forth the theme of 'separate Black identities' which are linked in one sense but are also divergent in another. Terry suggested that it was the 'Liverpool-born Blacks' who had the problems with coming to terms with their African and African Caribbean counterparts. He never mentioned that it could be the other way round also and that there could be problems between all of these groups. If I assess the entire interview I had with Terry, he did emphasise the 'scouser mentality' in many of the 'Liverpool-born Blacks'. That is, he argued that many of them had 'lost their roots' and had become assimilated into the dominant white culture in Liverpool. Some of them, according to Terry, had little interest in acknowledging their Blackness.

In considering this qualitative research in a holistic sense it appears explicitly that the respondents had no major psychological problems expressing their African heritage. Even Terry himself was very Black consciousness orientated. In a sense his remarks regarding the 'scouse Black' (a term for a born and raised Liverpool Black person) who is anti-African descent in character are something minor to the overall Black experience in the city. In other words, this is a case of personal prejudice and not something that is evident and emerging throughout the interview data. Nevertheless, Terry's views cannot be dismissed as irrelevant either, and there is certainly room for further sociological investigation.

Adrian Jefferies responded to the question of Black-on-Black social interaction in Liverpool and the issue of colour/shade in this manner:

> I think we're at a stage where [in the 1990s], . . . there is a problem over identity. Because if you asked someone from the older generation to describe themselves they'd gladly describe themselves as 'half-caste' . . . it's a term that they're very comfortable with, very comfortable with. To say to them that they're Black, they're offended with it. To a large extent, strange as it seems. Somewhere between the generations we've got a conflicting outlook on ourselves.

Adrian was asked to elaborate on why he thought there was a problem of identity among the older 'Liverpool-born Blacks'. He continued:

> what I'm saying is the 'half-caste boys' from a generation or two ago are more than willing to call themselves 'half-caste'. That's only applicable to their generation, say forty–fifty [years of age] plus. The opposite to that in terms of the multiracial communities, there's lots of Africans, Jamaicans and Somalis, for example, what do they think of local 'Liverpool-born Blacks'? . . . for want of expression, I'm forced to say 'half-caste'. They would not consider us to be Black. And I think they have difficulty in understanding why we persist in calling ourselves Black.

Adrian offers another insight into Black-on-Black interaction in terms of the generation gap in which the phrase 'half-caste' is more normalised and possibly less offensive to the older generation. Yet it is a term that is generally despised by the younger generation. He also points out the possibility of 'non-acceptance' by Africans and African Caribbean settlers, many of whom are, paradoxically, the fathers of the persons they would not accept to be genuinely of themselves. Is this theme a social reality? Do we need to acknowledge this paradox *within* the Liverpool Black experience? From the respondents' own testimonies it does seem apparent that the issue of colour/shade can have significance and in a sense helps shape an aspect of Black-on-Black social interaction. Regardless of the white racism faced by the entire Black community in Liverpool, it appears that internal conflict is also an important factor in determining the quality of life among multiracial descent persons.

David Jay gave this response to the question of colour/shade in terms of its relevance to the Liverpool Black experience:

I think it is [relevant] you know. I think to say that it's not is like being blind to it ... when we were growing up we used to give people stick [make fun] about each other, do you know what I mean? It was more in playing than any-thing else really. Things like 'darky' and 'light-skin', nothing more than that really.

I asked him whether he thought light-skinned Blacks received more social privileges over dark-skinned Blacks. He stated:

No I don't think that happens in Liverpool. I mean it was the 'half-castes' who got it bad in Liverpool, so that's why Liverpool-born Blacks was used instead. No you don't get privileged for being light-skinned in Liverpool, but you do get some joking over it among our own, do you know what I mean?

David stated that light skin in Liverpool does not confer so-cial status, as may well have occurred in South Africa or Jamaica under the apartheid regime and British colonialism respectively (see Chapter 4). This is an interesting point in relation to the global Black experience as it again emphasises the mutability of racial stratification. As in the city of Liverpool the experience of being 'light-skinned' has meant being associated to many negative stereotypes and extreme social isolation.[3] Yet in other societies having 'lighter' shades of skin has given a modicum of social privilege over 'darker' shades of skin.

Marlon Hasson suggested that he had never let the colour/

shade aspect of Black-on-Black interaction impact on him. He recognised that it exists within the Black experience in Liverpool, but he offered a rather philosophical explanation and perspective:

> the reason I say no is one, because when we say we're Black it's because we're non-white in that sense. And that's been a theme that most people have latched on to. However, when somebody else who is of a darker shade than me turns round and says you're white and you're not Black and so on, it seeks to educate each other, educate me in terms of OK we may all be Black, but we are all from different cultures. Erm being from different cultures, we do different things – Catholics do different things from Protestants. And what's there to say that just because we are Black that we have to be uniformed in that sense. So in many ways you take that as an education, but also it depends how derogatory people are in terms of what they're saying ... I would say they've been brainwashed by the white system, it's brainwashed them. I was having a discussion a few days ago with my uncle, a Somali, and we were talking about, as they would term us 'half-caste', which is 'half-breed' and so on, which is what we disagree with.

He continued,

> You re-educate them in terms of explaining how you feel. When we are the products of them and they are using a derogatory word ... we need to define that and make it clear to them who we are ... I am not here on my own, I have not brought myself here, out of thin air, I am a product of you and many other people marrying white women and having children, we are a product of you. Therefore my blood is your blood. Dilution of the skin is not a problem to me, it is the dilution of the mind that becomes the problem. And this is what I was trying to explain. Dilution of the mind in terms ... you can get a Black man who is abusive to me and this system has brainwashed him – that's a dilution of the mind. To me, erm, I find that very dangerous and it ultimately says what the system is about for me. You know, but the dilution of the skin [is irrelevant], it is what the blood contains.

Inadvertently, Marlon viewed the mode of behaviour within the Black community as being determined by the 'outside' or mainstream community. If Blacks do disagree among themselves then it was due primarily to either 'brainwashing' by the 'white system' or a lack of education, brought on again by the 'white system'. His understanding of anything socially unstable or dysfunctional in the Black community was due to external forces impinging on the potential unity of it. 'It is the dilution of the mind that is the problem, not the dilution of the skin.'

Terry Woan found it difficult initially to articulate the issue of Black-on-Black interaction, that is, in relation to the colour/shade of a socially defined Black person. This was not unique to Terry as it was a theme that came through in most of the interviews. Yet each respondent managed to provide some very personal and insightful comments, regardless of the sensitivity of the discussion. As Terry remarked:

> I know what you mean, but in the Liverpool sense it's hard to pin down. In my own way I've wished that I was 'full-Black' rather than being in-between. I don't know which road to go down, not being offensive to anyone, I'm half this and I'm half that. I just want to be one and be done with it. But again now I'm more confident of who and what I am and am happy to be what I am now. But in the past there's been quite a lot of confusion over them issues. I think we've always been seen as 'half-castes' in Liverpool, not so much now but it used to be, and nobody wanted them, they didn't belong anywhere, they were stray dogs [laugh]. They've always been seen as the 'English Blacks', the 'Liverpool-born Blacks'. The Jamaicans and Africans would say they've got the English ways, got no culture about you, you're just nothing [laugh]. You're just there, and you're not even white. It's like a stray dog kind of thing.

At the time of the interview with Terry his views above struck me as being rather deep, in a philosophical sense, yet painful. His articulation of what is happening in the terms of Black-on-Black interaction in the city of Liverpool was very penetrating. He had come to terms with how some Jamaicans and Africans may have negatively viewed his humanity, but at what cost? To think that some Jamaicans and Africans would deem a mixed origin person as a 'stray dog' speaks volumes for the dysfunctionality of the Black community. Whether Terry's view can be verified as being a commonplace fact is beyond the scope of this study. Yet how he put across the social interaction between Africans, Jamaicans and 'Liverpool-born Blacks', alone, needs further investigation by future social researchers. The views of the older women will now be considered in relation to Black-on-Black interaction.

c) The older women

Ada Hall had this to say about the issue of colour/shade in relation to the Liverpool Black experience:

> Well I've heard of it yeah, things like 'oh she's light or he's light'. But I don't think it applies much here in Liverpool. In America it's very strong. But I don't think it applies here.

In terms of her own life experience in Liverpool, Ada felt that the issue of colour/shade had not played a significant factor within the Black community. She related it more to the African American experience than life in Liverpool (since Ada had spent a number of years in the US). This again shows how racial stratification can be both a personal (subjective) experience and, at the same time, regionally specific (objective) to the respondents in this study.

Ada was asked to explain why it was that she used the US as an example. She said:

> I don't know, I think in America [North] there was a colour bar on, they'd try and pass wouldn't they? ['passing' means trying to pass as a white person in order to gain social privileges]. But in Liverpool that kind of thing is not common.

Unlike Ada, Emma Okuru had very strong feelings about Black-on-Black interaction in terms of how she felt some Africans thought about her and people of African mixed origin descent generally:

> Well us born in this country, they [Nigerians] have a name, I'm married to an Igbo man, I can't repeat it but I know it is a very insulting name. And I myself was insulted in my own house. And I'll never forget it.

She continued,

> The Igbo people have a big day in the New Year and they
> call it 'carrying the bones' were they remember the dead. You're
> supposed to give an account of what you've done through
> the year, what the children have done. How many children
> are born and all of this. As manager of the . . . club, my hus-
> band brought them back to the house, and they were very
> abusive. You see our people often play lip-service to us. Even
> though they borne us, some of them call us 'half-caste' and
> don't like us.

The depth of Emma's feelings during her account of her life
experience during our interview was quite profound. Due to her
high level of emotion I encouraged her to discuss the extent of
this aspect of Black-on-Black social interaction:

> Oh, ever since my husband died I've found it, I've found it.
> He was the son of a chief and he never told us. He never
> told his people in Africa about us. My son took us to Africa
> and we found this out. But let me tell you these Africans
> here in England do not like us, they do not like us . . . they
> don't like us because we know more about living here. You
> know my son found my husband's diaries, he was here from
> 1945 and for every year he had a diary. And in the diaries
> there's nothing about the kid's passing their scholarships or
> anything about them. It was all about the people outside there,
> all his Igbo people in Liverpool.

Did Emma feel in any way alienated from her husband's
African culture? She remarked:

> Well not me, but I've been made to feel apart from it un-
> fairly. I mean I cook the African food, I eat the African food,
> I brought my children up to respect African culture, but some
> Africans have shown a disrespect for me and my kids, that's
> wrong you see. Some of them don't like us who were born
> here. They did it very subtly but it was there.

The pain in Emma's feeling's of being in some manner 'rejected' by some Africans in Liverpool is clear. She indicated how

her African husband failed to tell his family in Nigeria about his wife and children in Liverpool. Neither to have been mentioned in the diaries of her husband clearly hurt her as she recalled the memory to me in our interview. Can Emma's experience be viewed as an isolated case? Or is this a common feature of the Liverpool Black experience which has not yet been unearthed to the degree that it should have been by social researchers? A number of the respondents, both young and old, implied that they felt somewhat alienated from their African parent. However, equally there were respondents who clearly acknowledged the love and respect that they received from their respective African parents. Therefore it is not possible to generalise Emma's case as being 'the norm'.

Indeed Doreen Kray's views in many respects defend Africans, while at the same time making sense of African Caribbean and African American 'cultural baggage' with respect to the issue of skin colour/shade in the Liverpool Black experience. She said:

I grew up in a situation were there was a lot of mixed race people and Africans, there were very few [African] Caribbeans here [in Liverpool], I'm talking about the late 1950s. [Being light-skinned] . . . wasn't relevant when I was growing up, the period when I was a teenager and growing up in the area. But, and this is the big 'but', and this is where I think there is a lot of confusion about it. For example, I think it's very important in terms of who you are talking to when you discuss this, to a person with a Caribbean background shadeism is a very traditional aspect of their cultural background. That was my experience both in Liverpool and in London. Now I went out with a guy called Winston [an African Caribbean man] and as far as I was concerned, his colour, the fact that his shade was the colour of my dad was insignificant to me. But when I started mixing up in parties and dances where there was a lot of Caribbeans there, I began to realise suddenly I was seen as a prize. And I remember one of his friends dancing with me and I was absolutely shocked because he said well 'you've got beautiful light skin', and I said 'what are you talking about?' It never actually occurred to me, as far as I was concerned I was Black or at least dark. And it wasn't an issue, the issue was racism. I was really angry with this guy, I didn't really like him anyway but that made it worse, but he was light-skinned and he suggested that I should go out with him you see. So there was all this sort of thing. He was actually a 'friend' of this guy I was going out with. And I began to realise that what all this 'shade-thing' was about in the Caribbean. I didn't realise that it was a thing to do with the whole culture of the Caribbean. When I went to London that's when it really hit me cos most of the Blacks were Caribbeans.

Doreen had much to say about colour/shade in terms of its relevance to the broader Black experience, but she felt that it was essentially a product of Caribbean culture. I asked her specifically to relate her experience of this phenomenon in the Liverpool context:

I think it had relevance in the Liverpool Black experience when they [African Caribbeans] brought with them this cultural baggage, but not before. It was also influenced by the Black Americans, I think we can't underestimate the influence of that. But I never found it in my own experience, because I was very active with Africans, I never found there was any ostracising of me because I was lighter coloured. What I found Africans did was when I said I'm the daughter of a Nigerian, they'd be so thrilled that I'd admitted it, they'd say well you're an African then. With Caribbeans it was much more complex. Some admired me cos I had light skin, some said 'oh you've got a white mother so you're not one of us'. The 'Black Power' types... All Africans I've met, and I've met an awful lot, I never found a problem over that, of all age ranges.

It is interesting how Doreen's experience of interacting with Africans is markedly different from that of Emma's. Whereas Doreen found Africans to be fully accepting of her mixed racial origins, Emma suggested that in her experience many Africans thought negatively about persons of mixed origin descent. Again this indicates how one cannot generalise too much about the overall experience of Black-on-Black interaction as it can be, in the examples of Doreen and Emma, very different depending on the Africans or African Caribbeans involved in the social intercourse.

Mary Ikem revealed how she had been called a 'yellow girl' by other Blacks when she was in the US with her African American husband. In view of this, I asked her to relate her experience of 'colour/shade' in relation to Liverpool:

> When I look back, you got the old African men, you know when you were kids, and they'd say 'you "half-caste" kids are too cheeky'. You didn't think nothing of that then in terms of shock and horror. But when I look back now it's a terrible thing to say. You know when you think about it . . . even now I hear some of the old African men now [stating the same phrase]. Now my husband [second husband], his country men [African Caribbeans] told him not to marry one of those 'half-caste' girls [in Liverpool] cos they're too cheeky . . . he said that men who'd come before him were saying don't marry them 'half-caste' girls – they're too cheeky. They cause too much trouble.

Mary was asked why it was that multiracial women in Liverpool got such a reputation, and she remarked:

> Do you know, I just don't know. I don't know. Maybe it was something like, people have this idea that maybe that, er, a union between a white woman and a Black man was seen as wrong and should never happen, so maybe the stigma of a child being born of this union, maybe it's something that's gone way back. Cos I mean like it's a taboo in the States and things like that, it was a taboo wasn't it? . . . So maybe it was that. That hangover of them days. That was classed if you were mixed race. You know there has to be something bad in that. Because in my childhood, most of all the people I know who had white mum's and Black fathers, there was nothing to say that these people caused trouble, they were all just nice people. Nice families you know.

Mary recalled the memory of childhood and how the older Africans 'in jest' spoke of the 'half-castes' being 'cheeky'. This recollection does reveal somewhat of a distance or 'racial space' between Africans and their children. Mary also recalled how her second husband was 'warned' not to marry a 'half-caste' girl from Liverpool by his countrymen, who were of African Caribbean origin. There is no mention of the colour/shade stratification of the Caribbean here. It is now a geographical demarcation which stigmatises the mixed origin female of Liverpool. The complexity of Black-on-Black interaction is again revealed in Mary's life experience. She herself had a wonderful relationship with her African father, one of mutual love and respect. Yet she can still relate to an objective, external experience of how Africans viewed her and other mixed origin persons in Liverpool. Again, at play here are the micro and macro relationships between Africans, African Caribbeans and 'Liverpool-born Blacks': there emerges a subjective and objective experience in the social interaction surrounding the issues of colour/shade, place of origin and so on, which cannot be generalised readily.

In point of fact when Jean Stevens was asked whether she felt colour/shade had any specific relevance to the Liverpool Black experience she pointed out:

> No, I think you can get a very white looking person with very African features, it never really existed as an entity. And from the people I knew there wasn't any justification in feeling that this is an issue to be reckoned with. My grandchildren are very, erm, light-skinned but they still feel that they are of the Black. We teach them to be proud of their Blackness, although they are very light and 'whiteish', they have to be proud and nobody can ever come to them and say 'you are an origin of a Black person', because they'd say 'I know and I'm proud of it'. So they've been taught that it's good to be proud of what you are.

For Jean, in her life experience in Liverpool, one's colour/shade 'never really existed as an entity'. She brings into consideration the fact that her grandchildren are 'light-skinned', yet are educated openly about their African ancestry. It is interesting how Jean does not recollect any division within the Black experience of Liverpool, given the fact that all the other 'older women' had something to say about the dynamics of Black-on-Black interaction. We will now turn to the views of the 'younger women' and gain an insight into how they consider this important issue.

d) The younger women

Anita Craven recalled a moment in her life which reflected on colour/shade within the Black experience:

When I was in the women's group, we went to do a talk in the university [Liverpool]. And some guy said 'you aren't Black'. And I said 'well we are Black'. Because this guy was very dark he said he was Black but we were not as we were lighter, I think he used the term 'half-caste'. So there was this big verbal fight and we said look 'it doesn't matter what shade we are, we are Black women'.

Anita was prompted to elaborate on how it felt at that moment, being rejected by another Black person, and she said:

I think the issue of getting to terms with 'who you are' and then him turning round and saying you're not Black, I think that's what upset everybody. We said 'hang on, what right have you got to say we're not Black?' I feel that at the end of the day if you feel inside, whatever shade you are, that you are Black, then you are Black. That's the way I see things.

Anita raises the issue of self-autonomy in relation to being faced with another Black person who denies her own Blackness. In a sense it also highlights the absurdity of 'racial labels' which manifest themselves in social interaction. Indeed, Anita in terms of the actual colour black is not *black*. Yet we could argue that this is no different from suggesting a white person not being actual *white* in colour. For instance, if you take a piece of white cardboard paper and glue it together back-to-back with a black piece, you could hold it up to a socially designated 'white' person (with the paper facing the white way) and see clearly that the 'white person' is indeed not white at all. The same can be done by placing the card next to a socially defined Black person (with the paper facing the black way). This is a lucid and quick exercise in showing how no person is really a specific 'colour' as such: it is only *socially constructed colouring* which takes place in our minds.

Diane Armstrong was encouraged to talk about her experiences of Black-on-Black social interaction, and whether or not colour/shade had ever impinged on her:

when I actually started seeing a darker guy, I actually overheard a girl, another Jamaican girl, saying to him 'what you doin' with that light-skinned woman?' You know, things like that . . . when I've been to dances, reggae dances, we used to get a few remarks and things.

Diane was then asked to explain how she felt about being talked about in that manner by another Black person and she retorted:

Hurt. It was worse than white people calling me a nigger. Because it was like your own not excepting you, I could expect white people not accepting me, but not my own. And because I see myself as a Black woman it hurts even more. You know what I mean? It hurts, it hurts a lot.

Diane also raised an important point which none of the other respondents touched on. That is, the rejection of 'darker-skinned' Blacks by 'lighter-skinned' Blacks:

I've actually sat down with a light-skinned woman who has said she'd never go with a man darker than herself. Yeah, I found it disgusting. It was more shock than anything to hear this woman talk like that. To me a Black man's a Black man, not whether he's light or dark. But there's obviously people who think the other way.

It is interesting to see how ardently Diane defends 'darker' Blacks even though she has herself been 'rejected' by some in the past. It gives an indication into the depth of racial consciousness she has. Earlier she pointed out how being rejected by 'her own' hurt more that 'being called a nigger by white people'. Like Anita, Diane has a strong conception of what it is to be both a woman and to be Black in a social sense.

Jean Williams also experienced the feeling of 'rejection' from 'darker' Blacks, although not openly:

It's not blatant, but I've had a few incidences, vibes, you know [from 'darker' Blacks] . . . and I'd say from more like Nigerian people who come here, I wouldn't say from the actually Liverpool-born Black people. I'm talking about the ones who've had the luck to be born in Africa. You know [laugh], they've come over here and you get the looks, you can see it. Especially if they know you're mixed, it's like their saying 'you're not pure'. It's amazing how the low level people get

on to. . . . You know, 'you're diluting the race', that kind of
mentality.

Jean was asked how she felt about receiving such a reaction
from other Blacks, having defined herself as a Black woman:

> It's really frustrating, it's like being in the middle sometimes,
> I mean where do you stand? Where do you stand? It's hard
> but I can only dismiss it and get on with who I am and as
> long as I know who I am that's all that matters at the end of
> the day.

Jean's response to 'rejection' is similar to those of both Anita
and Diane in the sense that she feels hurt, yet is still determined to acclaim the fact of describing herself as a Black woman:
'as long as I know who I am that's all that matters'. Her experience gives further indication that a number of the respondents
in this study have endured degrees of 'rejection' by other Blacks.
Jill Harlem was another respondent who had experienced the
issue of colour/shade within Black-on-Black interaction. She was
asked to give some examples of her experience:

> Two experiences, first of all when I went to visit America,
> people would not refer to me as Black. Everybody kept say-
> ing that I was white. And as much as I tried to explain that
> me mum was Black, her father was Black American, as far as
> they were concerned, regardless of any cultural experience, I
> was white. Because, features, I haven't got what you call 'Black
> features'. Even my hair, I haven't got what people refer to as
> 'Black hair'.

Jill was asked to describe her hair for me:

> My hair texture to me is European, dark and straight. That's
> what my hair is like. So to them [the African Americans she
> met] I was white. There was no arguing about it at the end
> of the day.

Jill says that on her visit to the US she experienced this 'rejection' from African Americans. This is strange considering that
there the 'one drop rule' still exists to a large extent, whereby

any amount of African heritage a person had would mean that he or she would be classed as an African American. In this regard, Jill was prompted to describe how she had been perceived by white Americans: 'to white Americans I was anything from Greek to African, to Asian, anything "Black", but not white. That was my experience in the States.'

Jill was prompted to give an account of her experience in Liverpool and whether her colour/shade and other phenotypical features had significance in her social interaction with other Blacks:

> more so over here, the Blacks that I've talked to and worked with and everything, to those who are of African descent and no immediate mix, they again have referred to me as not being Black. But even those who have got white mothers and Black fathers, yet have curly hair and dominant [Black] features, they've referred to me as not being Black.

As with Anita, Diane and Jean, Jill responded to the 'rejection' of her Blackness with proud defiance:

> I've got no interest in what other people refer to me as. For me, at the end of the day, as long as I know what I am, then I'm not going to waste my time justifying or explaining or sharing my knowledge and experience with them. Because these people have got their values and there's no way I'm going to change them. And if that's their belief they can hold onto them as long as they want, as long as I know who I am then I have got no problem with it.

Jill raised another interesting point in relation to Black-on-Black interaction which I had not heard mentioned by the other respondents. It relates to how some darker multiracial women have 'rejected' her Blackness:

> I've had it from Black women who've got stronger features, curly hair, and will say I am not Black. But yet have got white mothers and Black fathers. Or have got white grandmothers. Who have got white blood in them, close to their heritage, and they can say that I am not Black!

Again it is this apparent complexity of Black-on-Black interaction which reveals how absurd the social construction of 'racial types' can be. As Jill points out, even persons with similar mixed racial heritage to her own can be drawn into the 'I'm Blacker than you' syndrome. During the interview there appeared to be a deep frustration in Jill when she was explaining her experiences of 'rejection' by other socially considered Black people. In listening to the views of Jill and a number of the other respondents it does appear that, whether in the US or in Liverpool, the ambiguity of racial classification certainly seems to be a social reality inside and outside the confines of the Black community.

Some respondents were candid in their views on the theme of Black-on-Black social interaction. Indeed, apart from Mary Franklin, the younger women particularly had much to say on this topic. In the case of Mary, she did reveal to me that she felt somewhat 'different' from her 'darker' relatives. As to how this made her feel, she stated, 'as with white people, I did not feel good enough'. During the interview I attempted to get Mary to reveal why she did not 'feel good enough', but she was unable to continue because she felt upset about the topic. This gives an insight into the emotional pain involved in the respondents coming to terms with issues of Black identity. In this sense, it is usually a case in which the mixed origin respondent has to balance, socially and psychologically, simultaneously being both *inside* and *outside* of Blackness.

Is wanting to change one's physical appearance an issue?

Having considered Black-on-Black interaction and the issue of colour/shade within the Black experience of the respondents, we can now consider the theme of whether they have ever wanted to change their physical appearance. I wanted to try and assess the degree, if any, of 'self-hatred' and/or 'self-denial' among the respondents. I had read Toni Morrison's *The Bluest Eye*,[4] which considers the theme of Black self-hatred, and the idea occurred that this topic would give another understanding of the life experience of multiracial respondents, that it would complement the Black-on-Black social interaction theme.

Interestingly only 2 out of the 20 respondents admitted that they had thought about changing their physical appearance, and that was when they were children. The remaining 18 respondents, old and young, all informed me that they had never contemplated 'changing' themselves. Although the question did not outwardly refer to changing the 'racial side' of themselves, the majority of the respondents took for granted that the question referred to this. This is how Marlon Hasson reacted to the question: *have you ever wanted to change your physical appearance?*

> In my lifetime yes, I will be honest. It is an experience of which I can go back on. I remember at one stage when I was in Tiber Street School, because of the chasings and the beatings and those different things, my dad was a very peaceful man, however he chose not to be very informative. Whether this was because of my age at that time, I don't know, or maybe he didn't really understand. But I remember coming home one time to him and saying 'hey dad, what's a coon?' and he said 'it's OK son, don't worry about it, forget about it'. And it was brushed under the carpet and left. Erm I felt that I'd asked something wrong, he didn't shout at me, he just said there was nothing to worry about. I remember not long after that, because of the beatings, because of being different, because of being chased, praying at my bedside 'God will you please make me white tomorrow?'

Marlon was asked how old he was when he prayed to God to make him 'white' and he went on to state:

> Probably about eight or nine [years of age]. About that time, and I can always remember that, it sticks in my mind. And for me, I've children of my own now and they have a white mother as well, my aim in life is to have them understand everything in life I know. What I feel is to educate them to that, because they'll never be in that position [in the sense of not having someone to talk to about racial abuse]. They may be in a position then to tackle different things that they can't understand as they go through the years and learn from life. But in childhood, at least, I want them to be as stable as possible within the system. And it's about dodging different bits and pieces in the system, re-educating our children when they come home from school and sort of debriefing them in many ways . . .

There is a sense from Marlon's response that he did not want his own children to go through the experience he did in 'wanting to be white'. Therefore I wanted him to explain further how he had come from 'wanting to be white', to being a fairly 'Black conscious' individual who was now very proud of his racial origins. He remarked:

> There is so much locked up inside of you that you don't really know about, that you don't understand and don't know how to bring out. A whole lot of other people have felt the same, you have an outward appearance, but there is a lot locked up inside and you don't know how to release it. I think a lot of releasing came when I was in boarding school, erm, and a lot of the things happening there with the teachers being racist and things. You come to a stage in life, when you're coming to puberty and things when your mind becomes broader, and you say 'hang-on a sec, I am Black'! You know, and I'm not changing for anybody. You know, if you don't like me that's your hard luck. In many ways I think that that was a significant part, I couldn't wait to get back to Liverpool . . . What made me Black and proud? Again it was through that difficult school period and I could also see Black sportsmen achieving. You can go back to Muhammad Ali or John Conteh, and others, and you can see that they've got something that nobody else had – they are the best. They are the Champions, you know, and you always felt something inside.

Marlon explains his growth in pride as emanating from both a realisation of himself being Black and also through the success of Black sportsmen, such as the boxers Muhammad Ali and John Conteh. It is interesting to note that John Conteh is a native of Liverpool and also a person of African mixed origin descent. He became the Light Heavyweight Champion of the World in 1974. Marlon was an impressionable 15 years old at this time.

The self-hatred period in Marlon's young life could be interpreted as a negative reaction to his schooldays when he was at Tiber Street Primary School in Toxteth. He emphasised the problems of name-calling and, as a consequence, the fighting he endured in defending himself on a daily basis. This may have had something to do with him 'wanting to be white', as he saw it as an escape from the physical and mental brutality he was facing at school: *if he was 'white' he would be alright.* As he reached his teenage years he began to realise how futile it was to 'want to be white'. Instead he developed a racial pride, and having role models such as Muhammad Ali and John Conteh made him feel that he too could be somebody special – he connected with their Blackness.

In the case of Terry Woan, another young male respondent who admitted to having once 'wanted to be white':

> Like I said, when I was younger there was a time when I wanted to be white, and that's easy to recall because most of the images I received when I was about six was all about white heroes, the films you saw, the stars, sports and what have you. You saw more white people in work. All success was white. It all made me feel that it must be good to be white. I thought you'd get more money for Christmas presents, more money for houses, and so on.

In reply to this response, Terry was prompted to explain whether or not he viewed being 'white' as relating to social prestige or social status. If so, how did he then turn aside such thoughts and take up a strong Black identity? His reply offers another insight into the complexity of coming to terms with a mixed racial heritage:

> I just became aware of my identity that much more as I grew up, and dealing with the 'half-caste' thing of not having a home to call your own, type of thing. And then I came to the conclusion that I'd rather be full-Black than white. There's also a lot of things tied into that. Such as the Rastafarian history and Marcus Garvey. But there's a group in Birmingham called the Niabingi who don't see mixed race as being Black.

Asked how he felt about being 'rejected' by, for example, the Birmingham, UK, Black group Niabingi, he said:

> Disappointed really. There was a lot of contradictions within the Rastafarian religion, along with all religions. I mean they used Bob Marley, the Niabingi, yet he was a 'half-caste' so to speak. It's all a bit silly really.

Terry, in his quest for an authentic identity, realised growing into adulthood that 'being white' was not the answer. However, in coming to terms with his Blackness he also had to deal with the possibility of 'rejection' from other Blacks. Even though the Birmingham Black group that Terry refers to laud Bob Marley as a spiritual, cultural and political leader, they failed to recognise his mixed racial heritage. Yet, paradoxically, 'ordinary' mixed origin persons such as Terry would not be accepted as 'truly Black'. Is it any wonder that Terry refers to having felt he 'had no home to call his own' in terms of his Black identity? Nevertheless, from my understanding of our interview as a whole, he accepted the contradictions which exist in the 'Black community' and it is there, for better or for worse, that he posits his identity. Moreover, in my opinion, his struggle from a child to an adult, from 'wanting to be white' to 'wanting to be full-Black', is not yet over. Until he comes to terms with being an African of mixed origin descent he will no doubt continue to have problems coming to terms with his 'racial*ised* self'.

The fact that only 2 of the 20 respondents ever contemplated wanting to change their physical appearance may indicate a collective sense of racial pride. Jill Harlem, in her response, is testimony to the 'Black is Beautiful' legacy. When asked if she had ever wanted to change herself physically, she replied:

> Never, ever, ever. I've never wanted to change my appearance and I've never thought of wanting to be white. I've always wanted to be darker that what I am.

Jill was asked to explain why it was that she had always wanted to be 'darker' rather than 'white':

> I don't know, I suppose people, people, Black people who've had a bad experience at some stage have said that they'd love to be white. I've just always wanted to be darker. Cos it's so attractive. Black is just so beautiful and to be just that couple of shades darker would be, erm, perfection.

In response to her, it was put forward that the comment she made could imply that she was denying who she is by wanting to be a 'couple of shades' darker. She retorted: 'No, I think it's just a vanity thing. Black is just so beautiful. It's just so attractive and so appealing.' In many ways, Jill's position is inadvertently rooted in the 'Black is beautiful' consciousness era of the 1960s and 1970s. Although she said it was merely 'a vanity thing' in wanting to be 'darker', she still used the loaded phrase 'Black is beautiful' to explain her 'vanity' of wanting to be darker.

Adrian Jefferies was also very proud to be associated with his Blackness. In relation to the question of ever wanting to change his looks, his response was:

> No, in terms of appearance, you mean to look and act like a white man? No way, never. I'm proud to be Black! I certainly wouldn't want to change my appearance.

The majority of the respondents, just like Adrian, were proud of who and what they were in terms of their racial origins. This was something I was not readily expecting from the cohort of mixed origin respondents at the outset of this qualitative research. For example, I would have expected a greater number of the 'older generation' to have experienced feelings of 'wanting to be white'. However, it turned out that none of them were of that mentality: they were all 'proud to be what they are'. None would ever contemplate changing their physical appearance to look more 'white'.

Conclusion

This chapter has covered the themes of Black-on-Black social interaction and whether the respondents have ever thought about 'changing themselves physically'. The main objective of these two themes was to see how the issue of colour/shade within the Liverpool Black experience had particular relevance (e.g. as it has historically done in the US, South African and Jamaican contexts). In addition, there was an attempt to gauge the level of 'self-denial', if any, among the respondents in terms of their racial origins. Were they happy to be who and what they are: multiracial? Or would they rather be 'white' or 'darker'? These questions could not have been answered via theoretical postulation, yet they need to be examined in regard to the multiracial debates.

In terms of answering these questions, each of the respondents revealed some very personal thoughts from their particular life experiences. The comments surrounding the theme of Black-on-Black interaction and the colour/shade issue are particularly penetrating. The responses show the richness of the Liverpool Black experience. Indeed there is so much diversity among the responses that it is difficult to speak of the 'collective experience' of the respondents. Nevertheless there are a number of themes which have emerged and will be considered in the final chapter.

The point to make here is that many of the views differed markedly from respondent to respondent. In a sense one could see that their opinions were built on individual experiences and, as such, could not be readily generalised to all, or to the Black community as a whole. For example, a number of respondents had negative experiences with Africans while others had them with African Caribbeans. However, alongside these negative experiences were often loving and heartfelt *personal* relationships between the mixed origin daughter and African Caribbean father or African father and the mixed origin son, and so forth. There was no clear pattern of antagonism between, for example, Africans and 'Liverpool-born Blacks'. Only personal thoughts from the respondents that could not be deemed a 'collective' or uniform social experience due to the diversity of opinion.

The complexity of Black-on-Black interaction is made more evident if we again consider the view of Terry Woan, from the 'younger male generation', who saw both Jamaicans/Caribbeans and Africans as having a negative view of mixed origin persons within the city of Liverpool context. Terry's life experience led him to conclude that 'Liverpool-born Blacks' should be considered as the 'outsiders' in the Black community. This is a contentious issue which would require further research, as this study could neither confirm nor deny his point of view.

Emma Okuru, Mary Ikem and Doreen Kray all revealed the loving relationship they had with their respective African fathers. Yet Emma and Mary later explained that *some* Africans saw them and other mixed origin persons as 'half-castes', and that they were regarded as 'cheeky so and so's' by many. In a sense, then, there is both a 'personal' and a 'collective' way to understand more fully Black-on-Black interaction in the context of the respondents. It cannot be explained solely on the *personal* or the *collective* level; it is by understanding the *two* aspects of Black-on-Black interaction that we can gain further insight into this social experience. A rather salient point to acknowledge is that the respondents have a view of their 'racial selves', which is both personal (subjective) and collective (objective; that is, 'as seen by other Blacks'). This can be interpreted as a survival strategy on the part of the respondents. This strategy often includes a willingness or desire to overlook or suppress the negative aspects of Black-on-Black interaction, such as 'rejection'. The main problem for the respondents is 'surviving' in a dominant culture that is relatively hostile to *all* shades of Blackness.

In relation to the question of the respondents 'ever wanting to change their physical appearance', it was interesting to find out that only two of the respondents had ever contemplated it seriously. The two were of the 'younger male' cohort, and for one of them it was only a passing phase of 'self-hatred/denial' during his childhood years. For the other it involved a series of self-reflective phases in his life in which he tried to come to terms with his mixed origin identity. It seemed that Terry Woan had not yet reached the point where he felt entirely 'comfortable' with his racial origins.

The responses from Marlon and Terry as to the reasons why they each had thoughts of 'wanting to be white', reveal how painful it can be coming to terms with 'who you are' as a person of mixed origin descent. Crucially, however, it can be stated confidently that in regard to this qualitative case study of multiracial identity, 95 per cent of the respondents were 'happy with themselves' in a *physical appearance* sense and had never wanted to change who and what they were in a racial sense. Now, in relation to the social history of this multiracial population in the city of Liverpool context, this can be deemed a significantly positive research finding. It appears evident that the respondents are aware of themselves as being of 'mixed origin descent', but have found more than adequate strategies in coming to terms with what this entails in the social milieu of their lives in the city of Liverpool and broader British society. Chapter 4 will consider two other international cases in reference to the social construction of multiracial social groups: South Africa and Jamaica.

4
South Africa and Jamaica: 'Other' Multiracial Case Studies

> Without use of history and without an historical sense of psychological matters, the social scientist cannot adequately state the kinds of problems that ought now to be the orienting points of his studies.
>
> C. Wright Mills[1]

This chapter provides two brief international case studies of multiracial identity via the South African and Jamaican experiences. The two nations have particular histories that both complement and give contrast to an understanding of multiracial identity in the UK and US. In examining the social construction of 'race' in South Africa and Jamaica we shall see how racial labelling often acts as a useful mechanism in gaining social and economic power for one group at the expense of another.

In regard to South Africa and Jamaica historically, fundamentally it has been an elite white social group that held the lion's share of economic power. As economic might inevitably transfers to social power, it has also been predominantly white power structures that have determined, developed and structured the scope of racial labelling. By understanding this historical fact in the social construction of racialised groups we can make better sense of the contemporary sociological phenomena of multiracial groups. At bottom, in terms of multiracial identity, South Africa and Jamaica provide complex and intriguing historical case studies.

Before we consider South Africa as a case study a number of points should also be acknowledged in terms of the scope of a historical and sociological analysis. First, the focus here is primarily concerned with the development of the Cape Coloured community in South Africa and not of the entire population of groups that make up the society. Second, in following this course of inquiry, one can come to understand the structural position of the Cape Coloureds in relation to other population groups and examine how and why their status was socially engineered. Finally, the analysis herein should be viewed as introductory to an understanding of racialised relations in South Africa. Indeed South Africa is used as a case study merely to highlight the historical significance of racialised boundaries and multiracial identities in a global context.

South Africa and the social construction of 'coloureds'

The historical development of South Africa provides a useful case study in the social construction of 'race'. White settlers from Holland first occupied the Cape of Good Hope in 1652 and established a trading station via the Dutch East India Company. The main aim was to have a 'refreshing station for its Asia-bound vessels'.[2] The Dutch settlers formed sexual liaisons mainly with the indigenous Khoikhoi and to a lesser extent the San peoples. However, as the indigenous Africans proved to be difficult to tie down as servile labour, the Dutch in 1658 introduced the first enslaved Africans from outside the Cape area, who came from the eastern region, Madagascar.[3] This is the origin of the Cape Coloured population in Southern South Africa. Professor van den Berghe, analysing 'race and racism', states that, unlike the US, in South Africa 'Masters and house slaves lived together in the big house, played together as children, and prayed and fornicated together as adults.'[4]

At the outset of the development of the Cape colony there was less restriction on white and Black sexual relations. But by the end of the seventeenth century a rigid racial classification system had become embedded at the Cape and to a large extent it still exists today. Social control over Africans, via social exclusion, was a strong feature of white settlement in South Africa. Interestingly, however, when it came to the issue of sexual relations, a social distance was not rigidly imposed, as van den Berghe suggests:

Miscegenation in the form of concubinage between Dutch men and slave and Hottentot [Khoikhoi] women was quite common and no stigma was attached to it. Dutch boys frequently had their first sexual experiences with slave girls.[5]

Historically it is not something unique to have contradictions such as the one outlined above. Indeed even though miscegenation was severely and openly condemned up to and during the apartheid era, it nevertheless continued to be practised clandestinely. Accordingly the Cape Coloured population continued to grow, and under both the British and Boers (Afrikaners) they became a well-established intermediary group in South Africa. In other words, as a multiracial population they acted as a social buffer between the minority whites and majority Blacks.

In terms of the contemporary scene in South Africa, it offers a good example of the complexity of Black identity structure. In 1992 population statistics show that out of the 32 million inhabitants 73 per cent were African/Black (divided by Zulu, Xhosa, Sotho and Tswana); 3 per cent were African of mixed origin descent; 3 per cent were of Asian descent; with 18 per cent being of Caucasian (Afrikaner and British white) origin; the remaining 3 per cent of the population is unaccounted for.[6] Therefore in South Africa the white population are very much a numerical minority. Moreover, until the election of a democratic government in 1994, led by President Nelson Mandela, the whites held a virtual monopoly on both power and wealth. Apart from the exception of superficial and rather meaningless voting rights excercised by the Coloureds, all power was 'milky white'.

Under formal apartheid, 1948–94 (pronounced 'apart hate';[7] meaning 'apartness'),[8] the racial stratification was enforced by legislation which saw whites at the top, coloureds (usually meaning people of mixed origin – African and European descent) and Indians in the middle, with Africans/Blacks on the bottom. Each of these social group strata had differential access to social privileges and power. However, it was the white-minority which, by law enforcement and coercion, maintained the unequal social relations and kept a hold on the lion's share of power and privilege. For instance, under the system of apartheid African/Blacks, who make up the majority of the South African population, were not allowed to exercise their vote in elections, thus had no political power. In relation to the apartheid system Nelson

Mandela points out: 'The Population and Registration Act [1950] labelled all South Africans by race, making colour the single most important arbiter of an individual.'[9] Thus building on the past era of rigid racial stratifications, the architects of apartheid further consolidated the system.

Although the Population and Registration Act was revoked in 1991, destroying some of the key elements of apartheid, by the then President F. W. de Klerk, the history and legacy of colour-coding will not simply disappear overnight. Indeed it is embedded within the social fabric of society and undoubtedly a great effort is needed from future generations of South Africans to eradicate the negative effect of racialised classifications. An example of this continuing racial classification problem in the contemporary sense can be seen in relation to the uprising of the 'Coloureds' in a Johannesburg township. Violent street battles took place in February 1997 over the fact that the Coloured community felt socially isolated within the 'New South Africa' led by President Nelson Mandela. Here is how the UK's *Independent* newspaper reported the incident:

> The Coloured community feels hard done by. The complaint is that they were never white enough for the former ruling white Nationalists and now are not black enough for the ANC.[10]

This indicates the deep-rooted racialisation process in South Africa, whereby the reality of 'race' is highly evident in a social sense. Due primarily to social engineering by white Europeans (Dutch and British), via political and military domination over three centuries, South Africa is a profoundly and rigidly racialised society. It is something that manifests itself strongly in the present 'Coloured' social experience under the New South Africa, post-apartheid era. Regardless of the evident contradictions that the foundations of 'race relations' are built upon, South African multiracial persons are probably the most rigidly defined mixed origin group in the global context. This is due to the permanenance and stubbornness of 'race and racism' in the society's historical development. As van den Berghe writes:

> The ubiquity of race, the confusion between race and culture by the dominant group, and the latter's insistence that racial consciousness and 'purity' are essential to its survival

make South Africa a society ridden with conflicts and contradictions.[11]

It is the manifold contradictions regarding 'race relations' that continue to both baffle and intrigue the social investigator. Historically in South Africa multiracial persons have been placed within a supposedly distinct 'racial type' group. However, 'passing for white' is something that was highly prevalent among the 'Cape Coloureds' and it was not as difficult to undertake compared to the US. Indeed, unlike in the US, those South African multiracials who chose to 'pass' were often visibly African in terms of their features. The contradiction here is in the fact that Afrikaners turned a blind eye to those 'coloureds' who passed as long as they showed a distinct white character and had economic standing. As the historian George Fredrickson points out:

> The Coloreds who were most likely to 'make it as white' in the late nineteenth century were those who both came close to a not very exacting notion of European appearance and had some degree of wealth and education . . .[12]

The above contradiction is something that endured into the twentieth century, and the paradox of multiracial identity continued to infiltrate the 'pure white' South African identity. Again, as Fredrickson suggests:

> Clearly the tradition of a permeable color line that emerged during the days of the Dutch East India Company [in South Africa] persisted into the twentieth century – some would say even up to the present time – despite the growth of segregationist policies. The American 'descent rule' and official dedication to maintaining a fictive 'race purity' for whites were never an essential feature of South African white supremacy.[13]

Being 'white' in South Africa was ingrained with contradictions that the naked eye could easily behold. White supremacy was more difficult to achieve, however, because the white Afrikaner populace was only a minority. The US social structure could afford to be more rigid in regard to racial segregation due to the white population having a majority count. In South Africa the criteria for 'whiteness' were related more to class and cultural behaviour than skin tone and other phenotypical characteristics. The 'coloureds', for example, have largely an Afrikaner cultural background. As such, those 'coloureds' who have obtained a high degree of Afrikaner cultural capital may 'pass' into the white world of social privilege. However, the majority remain firmly rooted in a quagmire of social inequality.

This suggests how futile and absurd the actual social processes of white supremacy can be in regard to notions of racial purity. There is little scientific logic in considering any fundamental biological differences in the human family. Yet we can learn much from examining how societies have socially engineered racial exclusion to fit the needs of a dominant group.

In the case of South Africa, the specific function of the multi-racial population was inextricably interwoven with the numerical white Afrikaner cultural minority. Yet the Afrikaner minority held the overwhelming majority of social power and privilege in a Black nation for over 300 years. In this sense multiracial identity in South Africa has been forged to provide 'social breathing space' for the Afrikaner. The part, often unwitting or coerced, played by the multiracial population in the perpetuation of white supremacy, before and up to the end of apartheid in 1994, cannot be underestimated. However, in regard to social privileges, it is important to state that the multiracial population never gained little more than superficial concessions over the 'darker' African majority. In a prescient statement, before the fall of apartheid, and in regard to the social engineering of the multi-racial population group in South Africa, Fredrickson gives this account:

> The role of the Coloreds – currently more than half as numerous as the whites and about 10 percent of the total South African population – has inevitably figured in their calculations about the future balance of forces. Since there have been serious proposals in the twentieth century, even within Afrikanerdom, to coopt the entire Colored minority by granting them European status, or something very close to it, there may also have been a tacit agreement that absorbing its lighter members directly into the white group had certain demographic advantages.[14]

Although the 'coloured' population never actually were co-opted under the apartheid system, they were given a modicum of rights over the majority African/Blacks. It is this legacy of minor co-optation which may prove difficult for multiracial persons to escape in the New South Africa. Whether times have changed is debatable with regard to their assimilating into the larger African population. Reversing the past is not going to be easy for all South Africans. Those of multiracial ancestry will inevitably play an important role in deciding whether or not South Africa can shed its past and truly develop into a nation based on colour-blind democratic principles. This is a utopian vision as all indicators of the past and present point to further conflict over the issue of racial classification.[15]

To comprehend the social construction of multiracial identity in South Africa is to understand a prime example of racialised domination of one white group over a number of darker ones. It should also be pointed out that if the African/Blacks had been in ascendency then almost certainly those of multiracial ancestry would have 'passed' into this group rather than the white. The fact remains that white supremacy in South Africa, under both the Afrikaners and the British, produced a largely hostile and adverse social environment for the indigenous Africans. Therefore it was an inevitable corollary that those multiracial persons who could 'pass over' would ordinarily do so. This probably had little or nothing to do with self-hatred or 'identity confusion'. Rather it was the consequence of trying to survive more freely in a relatively unfree society. In this sense multiracial identity in South Africa should be theorised in relation to this powerful aspect of what could be termed: *coercive instrumental whitening*. Accordingly it is right to concede that were it not for social pressures in the subordination of Blackness, multiracial persons would probably not have sought the 'passing over' option.

Jamaica in context

The Caribbean island of Jamaica also represents an interesting case study of multiracial identity. Jamaica is a nation steeped in the heritage of enslavement and colonisation. The island was first inhabited around AD 650 by the Arawak Indians from the Orinoco region of South America. The Arawaks named the island

Xaymaca ('Land of wood and water'). Around 1400 a fierce people known as the Caribs arrived from the Guyana region of South America. The European-based traveller, Christopher Columbus, anchored at St Ann's Bay in 1491 and named the island St Jago, or Santiago, after St James. Briefly, in terms of its history with Europeans, Jamaica was a colony of the Spanish between 1509 and 1655, before being captured by the British, renamed Jamaica, and held by them from 1655 up to 'Independence' in 1962.

In a more contemporary sense, 1992 census statistics show that of the 2,450,000 Jamaican population, 76 per cent were solely of African descent; 15 per cent were of African mixed origin descent (mainly African and European origins); and the remaining 9 per cent were made up of Chinese, East Indian and Caucasian. Those persons who are of white European ancestry made up no more than one to two per cent of the overall population, while those persons with distinctly African ancestry allow for a majority 91 per cent.[16] The white population is a distinct minority in Jamaica.

However, the white population of European origins established a power-base in Jamaica first under the Spanish and later the British. They set up a social stratification system that had, in a way not too dissimilar to South Africa, a white hegemonic minority at the top. The labour market was therefore shaped in pyramid form with the major privileges being located at the apex. Professor Hoetink describes the early development of work patterns in this manner:

> A basic pattern evolved in which a tiny minority of whites (owners or overseers of plantations, some technical staff, colonial bureaucrats and clergy, large and small traders and their clerks, and some artisans) occupied the highest rungs of the social ladder (though they were internally divided into classes and factions according to wealth, education, and occupation).[17]

The development of a Jamaican society ingrained with social inequality was inextricably interwoven with the process of enslavement and colonisation. In both South Africa and Jamaica we witness the domination of a white minority over an African/ Black majority via the development of labour production systems. In terms of the relevance of skin tone, Hoetink points out the racialised stratification process:

The masses of slaves and their descendants were at the other end of the scale, while a mixed, colored section, although often desperately poor, received preferential treatment from the dominant [in terms of power] whites whenever there were intermediate jobs that no whites could or would take.[18]

It is important to point out that the 'mixed race' population were never accepted as social equals to whites in Jamaica. In time they were able to manoeuvre into positions of power and social privilege, but this was mainly during the post-independence era after the British had yielded sovereignty. Yet the development of a racialised society based on skin tone was firmly established and largely still exists today.[19] As with South Africa, Jamaica has a history of white European cultural domination; and it is the aspect of denying the humanity of Blackness which was a prominent feature of European rule. Colour-coding should be seen in this context as a social engineering process involving power relations.

The colour-coding hierarchy

Jamaica is renowned for its racialised colour-coding preservation, and whiteness is the pinnacle of all skin tones when one analyses the historical and sociological terrain. In regard to colour-coding and the 'racialising' of peoples by the 'white world', and under the rubric of white supremacy in the colonial context, the late and renowned Guyanese scholar Walter Rodney stated:

> Once a person is said to be Black by the white world, then that is usually the most important thing about him; fat or thin, intelligent or stupid, criminal or sportsman – these things pale into insignificance.[20]

He continues,

> The white world defines who is white and who is Black. In the USA if one is not white, then one is Black; in Britain, if one is not white, then one is coloured; in South Africa, one can be white, coloured or Black depending upon how white people classify you.[21]

In line with the South African and Jamaican contexts, for Rodney, a racial identity is often imposed on Black people whether they agree with the racial category or not. Where a given society is located, and the social dynamics which structure the 'race relations', have a major impact on the particular racial label attached to a given social group.

In regard to Jamaica, Louise Spencer-Strachan analyses the historical legacy of how the British structured, endorsed, promoted and legitimated a racially stratified society over a period of more than 300 years. She argues persuasively that there is a profound identity crisis among 'people of colour' and that this has had a devastating effect on the psyche of those persons who can claim African ancestry. Again, as with the South African context, social privilege has gone hand-in-hand with skin tone. As Spencer-Strachan states:

> The privileges that are afforded individuals in colonized class/ caste societies are predetermined by race and color: People who are lighter-skinned are close to the white ruling class, and as a rule are given preferential treatment.[22]

There is little doubt that Spencer-Strachan's perspective is correct in relation to the racialised societal structure that developed throughout the history of Jamaica.[23] In point of fact the noted nineteenth-century British author Anthony Trollope was one of the first writers to break down the Jamaican population by virtue of colour. He was an ardent racial supremacist and viewed Anglo-Saxons as a master people. In a book published in 1859 describing the social dynamics of 'race' in Jamaica, Trollope defined multiracial persons forcefully as 'coloured men':

> It is unnecessary to explain that by coloured men I mean those who are of mixed race – of a breed mixed, be it in what proportion it may, between the white European and the black African. Speaking of Jamaica, I might almost say between the Anglo-Saxon and the African; for there remains, I take it, but a small tinge of Spanish blood. Of the old Indian blood [Arawak and Carib] there is, I imagine, hardly a vestige.[24]

Social patterns of exclusion via skin tone remain a prominent feature in Jamaican life today.[25] Indeed the historical legacy of racial stratification, supplemented with social class, has had longevity in both Jamaica and South Africa. This phenomenon is also manifested in the sociological make-up of the contemporary scene in the two societies. Crucially, multiracial identity is born out of a sullied history of exploitation that is strengthened by an ideology of racism.[26]

Jamaica is a unique case study in the sense that the island originally was not home to indigenous Africans. Those Africans who came were first in chains and had been transplanted mainly from the West Coast of Africa in order to provide the labour for a largely plantation economy. It was under these conditions that a multiracial population began to emerge that was predominantly of African heritage, in a 'mixed race' sense.

Given this history it is little wonder the issue of miscegenation was for a long time a taboo subject. Indeed it is still deemed a relatively 'sensitive' area for the social investigator. Yet without an historical and sociological understanding of how colour-coding emerged and was perpetuated in Jamaica, the contemporary surveyor of 'race relations' would no doubt be baffled by the complexity of the light-to-black social matrix.

According to Spencer-Strachan, mixed racial origin Jamaicans, those with lighter skin especially, were 'brainwashed' by British colonialism to accept a pseudo-superiority over their darker brothers and sisters. As with the South African experience, this was something instigated by the white descendants of the British elite in order to divide and rule the majority African descendant Jamaicans. Spencer-Strachan maintains:

> Color-coding creates dissension and confusion among the group, and is an exploitative method to divide and rule: this divide and rule strategy is an old trick and has been very effective in many instances.[27]

Is it simply a matter of divide and rule? Or is it something that is born out of prejudice? The fact that lighter Blacks have at times been preferred over the darker is not necessarily something universal, for example, as shown in terms of the US and its 'one drop rule' (see Chapter 1). Yet it is difficult to dismiss the reality of lighter-skinned Blacks receiving a modicum of social privilege in Jamaica. The history of Jamaica, and its subsequent sociological unfolding in regard to the colour/shade of its inhabitants, clearly points to the maintenance of a divide and rule policy.

Conclusion

Although the above is merely an outline of the social engineering of multiracial identity constructs in South Africa and Jamaica, each case study gives us a greater understanding in how racial labelling can be formed and implemented via the social structure. South Africa is arguably the most severe case of how the practice of white supremacy was manifested through a false demarcation based on 'racial types'. Even though there emerged major contradictions in how persons were designated as either 'white' or 'coloured', the laws imposed upheld rather rigid barriers between the whites, 'coloureds' and Africans/Blacks.

Racial identity as a policy in South Africa constructed a distinct 'coloured' population. It is a multiracial population that has been moulded in a seething cauldron of social conflict via white racism.[28] In light of this fact it would be facile to ignore the inevitable social impact racial identity has had on the multiracial population group. Interestingly, the majority of studies involving the theoretical examination of 'identity politics' fail to show how the structural make-up of a given society, such as South Africa, often determines a person's racial identity. Instead these studies tend to rely on the accounts of contemporary persons and fail to deal adequately with the historical and sociological backdrop of the society of which the individual is a product.[29] In point of fact it is the complex interrelationship and intersection of biography, history and society that proves useful in understanding the dynamics of multiracial identity constructs. Again, as the late and noted sociologist C. Wright Mills suggested:

> Social science deals with problems of biography, of history, and of their intersections with social structures . . . The problems of our time – which now include the problem of man's very nature – cannot be stated adequately without consistent practice of the view that history is the shank of social study.[30]

It is important to note that if biography is shaped by history and the given society, then it is logical to infer the same for multiracial identity constructs. Just as we cannot divorce the way a person is socialised in her identity development, the given society itself has to be considered. South Africa is certainly a society primed in the historical vicissitudes of racial inequality and domination. In view of this insight social history should not be dismissed as something superficial in the assessment of multiracial identity. Indeed it is a crucial aspect in relation to how a person becomes aware of her place in a society that is highly 'race' conscious.

Jamaica as a multiracial case study is useful inasmuch as it shows how the displacement of Africans from Africa to the Caribbean island was the beginning of an essentially interracial population group. Too often scholars ignore this historical fact and tend to see the Caribbean region as something unique and thoroughly indigenous. Yet the multiracial population, which accounts for the majority in a sense, have ancestral origins in from Europe, Africa, India, South America and China. However, in Jamaica it is mainly European and African interracial coupling that is dominant in terms of multiracial heritage.

A society retaining British colonial remnants of racism and classism, Jamaica is today a relatively poor nation and to a large extent still riddled with intragroup colour/shadeism. Although the situation is not as bad as it once was under the yoke of British colonialism, Jamaica is still very much a colour conscious society. Professor Barry Chevannes, from the University of West Indies at Mona, Jamaica, suggests that the deep-rooted nature of colour stratification still prevailed in an ideological sense and this is manifested in the social structure. 'It prevails in certain kinds of aesthetics and there is a public perception that white or light is good.' In other words there is a public conceptualisation that grades colour from the preferred white down to the unpreferred Black. Professor Chevannes maintains that this light colour preference is also manifested in the social structure – one rarely comes across a poor white person in contemporary Jamaican society. He contends that if a white person is poor then a little education would see him or her climb very rapidly up the social ladder. However, this would not be the case for a dark-skinned or Black Jamaican.[31]

Despite the passing of time and the end of British colonial rule there still lingers the aftermath of racism and the notion of white supremacy. Even though many thousands of Jamaicans could claim 'white British' heritage, if a person of colour does not have the 'right' skin tone and hair texture life will inevitably be more difficult in terms of receiving social equality and opportunities for upward mobility. In a sense, multiracial identity is relative to the number of racial characteristics that match the subordinate group – in this case those of African descent. The closer one is to the Black African phenotype, the more likely one is to be socially excluded in Jamaican society. Whiteness still appears to be the favoured phenotype. Crucially, in Jamaica multiracial identity is forged between the polar opposites of black and white, and somewhere between these opposites lies a person's, often imposed, social identity.

Another important lesson we can learn from the multiracial experiences in South Africa and Jamaica is the way an individual is constrained by the social structure of society. Indeed human agency in the determining of one's social identity is little more than relative in these societies. Social positions, such as employment, appear to be largely won via racialised identities and not enough by the individual's own effort, talent and self-determination.

In South Africa, for example, there is a diverse division of labour that has been historically based on either skin tone or one's racially designated position in the society. An African/Black who was particularly gifted in a professional sense would not have been able to aspire due to the prevalence of social inequalities in regard to employment opportunities. The same can be said in relation to Jamaican society, where group membership and specific social privilege are again primarily determined by skin tone, rather than ability and individual merit. Therefore to be of multiracial origin in South Africa or Jamaica has tremendous consequences in terms of one's social identity. Self-identity is often imposed on the individual by the social structure, regardless of how a person may agree or disagree with the definition. Crucially, being labelled a 'coloured' in South Africa or a 'high brown' in Jamaica has tremendous social significance.[32]

Instructive in this sociological phenomenon is the fact that human agency appears to be acutely constrained by society. This is not to suggest that being confined to a specific social group prevents social actors from 'escaping' or 'passing' into another group. Of course humanity's conscious and self-conscious ability to think and create will always find alternative avenues to escape social oppression. Nevertheless, the constraints on multiracial persons are and have been in South Africa and Jamaica highly significant at the macro level in their respective social worlds.

On a micro level notions of the 'self and identity' will no doubt differ from person to person. Depending on the society, however, it is the level of social closure in operation that may well determine the importance in being part of a particular group. South Africa under apartheid can be viewed as a totalitarian state where racial grouping was something ingrained in the distribution of power and resources. The apartheid regime, supported by an overt doctrine of white supremacy, gave concessions to the 'coloureds' only to cultivate and enhance the system itself. Therefore on a micro level being 'coloured' meant not being African/Black, and this label allowed a modicum of social leeway. The possibility of a less harsh quality of life in an openly racist society is often all the incentive a person needs to opt out of a stigmatised social group. Again this is an example of how the social structure (macro level) effectively determines the behavioural outcome of the individual or group (micro level). Yet the paradox remained, in that those 'coloureds' who accepted the concessions, and most had little choice in the matter, from the apartheid regime were still effectively buying into the notion of their own racial inferiority in relation to the socially designated white populace.

The complex and changing forms of racism in different societies on one level prove extremely difficult to conceptualise. Yet if, for example, multiracial identities are examined from both a historical and sociological perspective it helps clarify the contemporary structuring. This chapter provides merely an insight into the way in which South Africa and Jamaica have developed multiracial populations under the umbrella of white supremacy. To understand multiracial identity in these nations one ought to trace Afrikaner and British colonialism with each of their concomitant racialised ideological themes espousing superior/inferior 'races'. In this sense, future empirical investigations using a historical and sociological context will prove rewarding in the analysis of multiracial identity in South Africa and Jamaica. The following chapter will assess both the reality and relevance of socially constructed multiracial identities.

5
Assessing Multiracial Identity

The African Diaspora(s) in general and the English-African Diaspora in particular remain fertile ground for the cultivation of an orphan consciousness. An orphan consciousness emerges when one does not grow up with one's natal parents or kin – in this case 'Mama Africa'.[1]

Jayne Ifekwunigwe, a contemporary anthropologist, writes above in relation to the displacement of the multiracial person in the African Diaspora. Underlining her analysis is a perspective which views the mixed origin individual as a 'victim', psychologically tortured, forlorn and deserted. Rather than searching for a bygone past in claiming a mythical African-centred identity, she maintains that it is better for mixed origin persons to create a new social space. The specific and rich social histories should be focused from where they are. In doing this, mixed origin persons can relieve themselves of an 'orphan consciousness'.[2] In her analysis, Ifekwunigwe fails to explain the complexity of, for example, a South African 'coloured'. Indeed a multiracial person from South Africa indigenously belongs to 'Mama Africa' and therefore is not an 'orphan', as in Ifekwunigwe's African Diasporan sense. Yet regardless of the limitations of her analysis, Ifekwunigwe provides a useful theme to keep in mind as we navigate the complex reality of socially constructed multiracial identities.

In societies with a tradition of overt racialised stratification, such as the US, South Africa and Jamaica, it is not too difficult to assess the reality and relevance of multiracial identity. Yet in relation to the UK it is a little more complex due to the lesser number of so-called Black 'ethnic minorities' in relation to the overall white population. Again this fact indicates that it is important to understand each multiracial experience in its own right. Indeed, how far is the UK experience different from that of the US? Or how similar or dissimilar is the South African experience in relation to Jamaica? What in common have the UK, US, South Africa and Jamaica in terms of their social construction of multiracial peoples – that is, of mainly European and African origin? These questions will provide the basis for the assessment of multiracial identity in this chapter.

In following this path we will assess both the reality and relevance for the social construction and status of multiracial identities. In addition, drawing from the work of the sociologist F. James Davis, we will consider why it is that one multiracial status may well be distinct and yet another rather blurred in a given society. This is certainly the case in regard to South Africa and the US respectively. In terms of the UK and Jamaica, these societies again differ somewhat in terms of how their multiracial social groups have developed. However, for all their diversity, the multiracial populations discussed here have one thing in common: a relationship to white European supremacist thought and practice. It is necessary to assess how this interlocking international history has impacted on multiracial communities.

White supremacy and multiracial identity

In assessing the notion of multiracial identity and social grouping it is worth noting how it has been inextricably linked to the ideas of white supremacy. Peter Fryer maintains that the rise of pseudo-scientific racism in the UK was interwoven with that of the British Empire and its dominance of the darker peoples of the 'New World', especially during the eighteenth and nineteenth centuries.[3] With the UK being a nation that espoused the virtue of Christianity via the growth of the British Empire, it needed to excuse itself from the obvious inhumanity that follows in the path of racial dominance and oppression. Put simply, imperial theorists espoused a justification for the enslavement and genocide[4] of Black peoples through an array of pseudo-scientific assumptions expressing the innate superiority of white Europeans over Africans and Asians. Indeed, to have any degree of African ancestry was also to possess, according to European racialist theories, inferior human qualities.[5]

The historian George Fredrickson, in his ground-breaking book *White Supremacy,* suggests that white supremacy refers to the attitudes, ideologies and associated policies connected with the development of white European domination over 'dark' populations. He maintains:

> white supremacy means 'color bars,' 'racial segregation,' and the restriction of meaningful citizenship rights to a privileged group characterized by its light pigmentation.[6]

When examining the issue of multiracial identity it is important to understand the legacy of white supremacy. It is a theory and practice based on the irrational opinion that white Europeans (mainly of Anglo-Saxon and Northern European origin) are inherently superior to non-Anglo-Saxon origin peoples – particularly those of African and Asian ancestry. Moreover, it is also a theory and practice that hover over the subject and analysis of miscegenation. Absurd as it is, we have an approximate 500-year history of European domination and subjugation of African and Asian peoples, yet wherever Europeans have colonised they have sexually intermingled with the indigenous populations. Apart from this obvious paradox, it is a taboo subject that should be exposed, yet rarely does this occur in an academic sense.[7]

Charles Mills, a professor of philosophy, has recently examined how traditional European philosophy refuses to acknowledge its relationship to the development of white supremacy. For Mills, 'White supremacy is the unnamed political system that has made the modern world what it is today.'[8] In other words it is a system that has been developed over centuries of European global expansionism and domination, but in mainstream philosophy and ethics it is taboo subject matter. Mills further contends that the issue of 'race' is segregated from 'the world of mainstream (i.e., white) ethics and political philosophy.'[9] This manifests itself in a number of ways, but specifically it is in the exclusion or offhand dismissal of 'ethnic minority philosophy', for want of a better phrase. It is the manner of legitimating, making 'normal', the inferiority of dark peoples that Mills is alluding to. Without careful consideration of how the 'white world' has been shaped and formed through its intellectual heritage, understanding the various constructions of racial identity will inevitably be that much more complex.

Time and again contemporary studies fail to deal with the history of white supremacy in terms of connecting it to the contemporary sociological aspects of multiracial identities.[10] Yet the notion and practice of white supremacy cannot be dismissed as something ephemeral or superfluous to the history and social construction of multiracial identities. Indeed at the heart of the culture of racism in societies structured in racial dominance is this historical legacy of white supremacy. Take, for example, the view below of the ex-Prime Minister (1979–90) of the UK, Margaret Thatcher, with regard to what Europeans have in common historically:

> Too often the history of Europe is described as a series of interminable wars and quarrels. Yet from our perspective today surely what strikes us most is our common experience. For instance, the story of how Europeans explored and colonised and – yes, without apology – civilised much of the world is an extraordinary tale of talent, skill and courage.[11]

Margaret Thatcher displays an overt notion of white supremacy in her perspective of European colonialism. However, an integral aspect of European expansionism relates to the issue of its miscegenation with, using Thatcher's anaylsis, the 'uncivilised' humanity that it came into contact with. Taking this into account, it would be facile to confine the semantics surrounding multiracial peoples to that of a contemporary phenomenon in suggesting that such persons are, for example, 'new people' and ahistorical (see Chapter 1).[12] European racist ideology and jingoism, as advocated by Thatcher, is a significant backdrop for appropriate comprehension and analysis of racially mixed international communities.

Therefore, to assess multiracial identity in the UK, US, South Africa and Jamaica in a sociological sense demands both a regional and historically specific analysis. Each nation has its own peculiar social relations when it comes to multiracial populations. With regard to the UK, we have in this study gone beyond the theoretical and provided empirical evidence via in-depth interviews with multiracial respondents of African and European origins. What emerges from the collective views of the mixed origin respondents is that they seem to grasp both a personal and a societal understanding of their multiracial identities. In addition each articulates how they manoeuvre through the incongruity of racial labelling to the reality and relevance it has to their social existence in Liverpool, England.

It is this 'personal' and 'societal' dichotomy that needs to be highlighted when we assess multiracial identity constructs. Despite the fact that many persons could openly claim to have a number of racial origins, from the UK research it was found that the majority of the respondents regarded themselves as 'Black British' (see Chapters 2 and 3). We could take this to mean 'Black *and* British', where 'Black' represents the main aspect of one's social life, and 'British' accounts for the amalgamation and influence of this specific diasporan experience. Or maybe it is a term employed in order to move away from the negative status labels associated with multiracial identity in the UK (see the Glossary).

Social status and multiracial identity

Given the reality of white supremacist ideology in negatively labelling multiracial persons, F. James Davis has put forward seven types of statuses found around the globe. Davis suggests the following ways in which multiracial groups have been, and are to some extent, viewed in certain societies:

> Racially mixed progeny may have (1) a lower status than either parent group, (2) a higher status than either parent group, (3) an in-between marginal status, (4) a highly variable status, depending more on social class than color, (5) a variable status independent of racial traits, (6) the same position as the lower-status group, and (7) the status of an assimilating minority.[13]

Davis found that the above statuses of multiracial groups relate to specific aspects of a racialised identity in certain societies. Interestingly, he maintains that in Uganda, east Africa, the multiracial persons among the Ganda people are largely viewed with 'condescension and contempt', and are also rejected by white society.[14] This is contrary to the situation of the South African 'coloureds', who were traditionally used as a buffer group by the ruling white minority and rewarded with a modicum of social privileges over their darker brothers and sisters. Davis gives the examples of other multiracial groups around the world to substantiate his analysis. A similar 'bottom-of-the-ladder' status falls to the Métis in Canada (usually being a mixture of French or Scottish and native Indian women), the Anglo-Indians in India, Korean-Americans in Korea, and Vietnamese-Americans in Vietnam.[15] These groups represent the worst possible scenario for multiracial persons, as they are classed 'as a separate and debased people' in their respective societies.[16]

In relation to a multiracial group having a higher status than either parent group, Davis points to the historical experience of Haiti. Having been inspired by the French Revolution of 1789, the enslaved Africans and so-called 'mulattos' successfully rebelled and won their independence from France in 1804. While prior to the revolution the free 'mulattos' were an intermediate social group, as in South Africa; after it they emerged as the economic and political elites. Their hegemony was shared, however, by elite members of the majority Blacks. Yet the 'mulattos' held on to the main reins of political and socioeconomic power. Davis maintains that the 'mulatto elites' 'look down on unmixed blacks and despise the small white population.'[17]

This specific experience of a multiracial group in Haiti can be seen as another racialised social group. This time it is a multiracial experience fashioned under the yoke of French colonialism. The 'mulattos' incongruously ascended to power in a society based and nurtured on the tenets of white supremacy. Indeed the social framework in Haiti developed deep divisions and antagonisms between dark and light brown under French colonial rule. This legacy survived beyond independence and is still, according to Davis, a prominent feature of Haitian social relations.

There is no need to elaborate on Davis's third status, as we have discussed in Chapter 4 an example of a multiracial social group that has an 'in-between' status via the South African experience. In addition, Davis's fourth model status is typical of the other case study we have discussed in terms of Jamaica and its colour-coding societal structure. It is a racialised structure that also involves the issue of class – a remnant of British colonialism. In line with Davis, it is fair to suggest that both skin tone and economic standing are still crucial determinants in one's opportunities for upward mobility in the majority of the

Caribbean Islands,[18] those once held and culturally dominated by Europeans.

Davis maintains that in Hawaii racially mixed persons represent the majority populace. Unlike the Caribbean and Latin American region, there is no specific colour-coding embedded within the Hawaiian social structure.[19] Davis suggests that it is probably due to multiracial persons in Hawaii being in the majority. Using 1980 census data he reveals that 33 per cent of the population designated themselves as 'white' in terms of their racial identity; less than 2 per cent regarded themselves as 'Black'; while the majority 67 per cent stated that they were 'other'.[20] Again this indicates the absurdity of racial labelling, while at the same time revealing the deep significance it has even in a relatively equality-based society.

In terms of Davis's sixth status model, multiracial persons having the same social status as the subordinate group, he uses the example of the US to illustrate his analysis. He regards this as the 'one drop rule' or 'hypodescent' which basically assigns all such persons having African ancestry to the African American community. This is the reality of the US racialised social structure. Moreover, even though the average member of the African American community could pass for 'coloured' in South Africa, he or she is deemed to be 'Black' in America.

From my experience of conducting interviews with multiracial persons in the UK context (see Chapters 2 and 3), it is my opinion that the one drop rule also relates to the city of Liverpool context. Indeed considering the above statuses it is the one drop rule that is most appropriate in describing the UK experience. This may well be due to both the US and UK having majority white populations and there being no need for a buffer social group in the racial sense. Having a numerical majority, a white population does not need to introduce elaborate and fanciful racial classifications. Certainly in relation to the UK, it is often simply 'not being white' that demarcates the various minority Black communities. There has been no historical 'divide and rule' via colour-coding in the UK and this is probably because there has been no need to do so. However, in the British colonies the need for a racialised hierarchy was due to there being a white minority population.

Racialised stratification was a required feature under colonial policy for *white* South Africa and Jamaica as the respective white populations were distinct minorities. Therefore, when there was a need to produce an intermediate group, such as the 'coloureds' of South Africa, the white colonial power structure developed one. Yet with a majority white population, as in the UK and US, there is little need to introduce such an intricate racialised system. This is not to suggest that at the micro level colour hierarchies do not occur in societies with a majority white population, indeed they do but have only limited influence when not backed forcefully by a white power structure. In short, colour/shadeism can operate at the intragroup level, as it has historically occurred in the US.[21]

Professor Davis's final status model for multiracial persons is termed the 'assimilating minority'.[22] He refers to those multiracial groups that have been incorporated into the life of the dominant community. Writing from the perspective of the US, he argues that many Native Americans, Japanese Americans and Filipino Americans fit this category. Alluding to the melting pot theory Davis maintains:

> Throughout American history the pressure has been heavy for the native Indians and all newcomer groups to adopt the dominant Anglo-American ways and beliefs.[23]

Davis goes on to suggest that the assimilation process has often been a two-way phenomenon whereby minority cultures have reciprocated in kind to the dominant Anglo-Saxon culture. For example, certain foods that originate from minority cultures in the US are now mainstream validated: Chinese, Mexican and Japanese foods fit this criterion. In short, for Davis, if non-Anglo-Saxon cultures shed their 'old ways', for example, their mother language, and learn American English, Anglo-American history and so on, then they can eventually assimilate into the mainstream Anglo-Saxon culture – at least in theory. Davis admits that even these multiracial groups have faced tremendous discrimination in the US, but it is possible to eventually assimilate over a period of two or three generations.

Davis's seven status schema is instructive in giving an insight into the various ways multiracial groups have had their group identities socially constructed in certain societies. Assessing the phenomenon of multiracial identities is not an easy task in a contemporary sense. But with an understanding of 'white supremacy' in relation to 'New World' peoples there is greater clarity in examining international multiracial experiences. Despite the complexities involved in establishing a logical pattern of meaning to this social experience, the notion of racialised and cultural domination over lands and peoples, through the white European colonisation of the 'New World', appears to answer many of our questions. In point of fact, each of Davis's status models of multiracial groups has a relationship to white supremacy, especially in terms of how it has indirectly determined intragroup relationships in Black communities. This is a key theme in the assessment of international multiracial identities.

Nomenclature default and multiracial terminology

It is difficult to deny the large effect which racialised labels involving multiracial persons have on the social construction of their identities. Historically, as shown above, we have numerous societies that developed rather offensive nomenclature to describe multiracial persons. Again, in assessing the aspect of multiracial identity in an international context, we need to associate it within the context of white supremacist thought and practice. Indeed, it is out of white European philosophy and intellect that the origin of such labels as 'half-caste', 'half-breed', 'mulatto', and the many more, emerged (see the Glossary for more detail).

The social fact remains that most of the labels associated with multiracial peoples are in some form problematic. In a sense social analysts often unwittingly fall prey to the racism and mythology by accepting such racialising uncritically. Yet it is rather difficult to navigate through the historical and sociological remnants of specific racialised contexts without being bogged down by imperial nomenclature. Moreover, despite the proliferation of 'identity politics' in the academy, little has been achieved to enhance clarity. It is fair to suggest that there has been an increase in the nebulous aspect of 'Black identities' via the use of ever-confusing terms.

Ifekwunigwe offers a good example of the contemporary confusion in racial labelling theory. Her research is in relation to UK multiracial persons of African and white European origin, yet she prefers to use the term 'metis(se)' (metis, masculine, and metisse, feminine) when defining such persons. Ifekwunigwe states:

[metis(se)] is the French-African term I have chosen to describe project participants all of whom have British or European
mothers and continental African or Caribben fathers.[24]

The above definition of a specific multiracial group in the UK
is somewhat confusing as it comes via a French-African experience. Ifekwunigwe is very critical of Afrocentric scholars for not
discussing the relevance of African diasporan experiences in and
of themselves. For example, the English-African diaspora in the
UK and the US-African diasporan experiences each represent
unique communities, even though they both have cultural ties
to the African continent. Social researchers, according to Ifekwunigwe, need to acknowledge this complexity and not get drawn
into simple anaylses viewing the African diaspora as monolithic.
However, in this criticism Ifekwunigwe unwittingly contradicts
herself. On one level she states that it is important to understand the experience of multiracial persons within the context
of their Black cultural roots, along with the respective 'host nation'
experience. While in relation to her research in the UK, she
defines the multiracial cohort under French-African terminology! This confusion is typical of a number of contemporary
'identity politics' analyses. It seems that academics are forever
searching for nomenclature that is 'new' in order to provide
something original in the research output. But often the result
is to merely bring forth another syncretic, and obscure, term
for describing multiracial persons.

Ifekwunigwe is correct to point out the need to understand
each multiracial experience, via the African Diaspora, in its own
right. As a matter of fact it is certainly a key theme in this
study. Yet, and this is the main problem with Ifekwunigwe's
perspective, it is equally important to analyse the links and similarities of international multiracial experiences. If we overlook
this interwoven aspect of multiracial identity, then the research
findings will be severely lacking – especially in the case of
African diasporan experiences.[25] Simply applying 'new names'
to multiracial persons in the UK, in the aim of providing an
anti-essentialist analysis, fails to adequately deal with the actu-
ality of 'not being white' in a white dominated society. This
lived reality usually entails being called a 'nigger' for persons
born of mixed African and white European origins (see Chapters 2 and 3). In view of the catalogue of anti-essentialist tracts

emanating from postmodern 'Black' theorists, such as Ifekwunigwe, it would be refreshing for them to note this important social fact. Too often the obvious aspects of multiracial identity are ignored for a more evasive, intricate and turgid analysis.

The problem of nomenclature continues to be one of the main aspects of multiracial identity theory. Even though the fact of Blackness goes beyond the realms of skin tone and hair texture, being of 'mixed origin' descent can provide a means of dividing Black peoples.[26] This begs the questions: what's in a name? Is it a significant aspect of identity? Considering this assessment of how international multiracial communities have emerged and developed, there is little doubt that 'a name' is very important. Indeed from the perspective of the UK, US, South Africa and Jamaica, we can see how racial labelling, based primarily and incongruously on phenotype, has produced various racialised social relations within these societies.

Naming is therefore central in the assessment of international multiracial identities. In addition, regardless of the various social circumstances in which racialised relations have developed, it appears evident that the naming and classification of international multiracial groups is interwoven with upward and downward social mobility. Societies structured on racialised populations will no doubt continue to manifest social inequality due to the deep-rooted nature of racism.

Take South Africa, for example: there is little optimism that the rigid racial demarcation will subside in the near future given the current social indicators. Racial boundaries were firmly embedded under the white-minority apartheid structure. In view of this it could take centuries before a genuinely 'colourblind' society emerges.

Along with a demarcation of humans based on phenotype, we should not underestimate the relevance of economic power. In Jamaica, the dark-skinned Blacks who have gained financial strength are beginning to make limited strides in the society, but they are relatively few in number. As such, wealth and the power that comes with it is primarily still in the hands of the minority white and light-brown skinned Jamaicans.[27] Social privilege is in effect linked to skin tone and generations of Jamaicans are associated with this societal formation. It would be fanciful to assume that this situation is going to change in the near future. It took hundreds of years to establish a white cultural hegemony in Jamaica, and so it will be for its demise.

In terms of the US and multiracial identity, the long history of the one drop rule and the fact that any amount of African ancestry means a person is 'Black', show again how societies adopt different racialised schemata to fit the presumed social needs of those who hold the majority power, in this case whites. There is little doubt that the US provides a complex cultural history of racialised domination in regard to its African American population particularly.[28] That history that is also interwoven with miscegenation, and being 'Black' in the US can actually mean looking 'white' at times.[29] The contradictions are profound in the US concerning the racial domination of whites over Blacks and other 'peoples of colour'.

There is, for example, very strong evidence pointing to the fact that Thomas Jefferson, the leading Founding Father of the US, sired five children with his African American slave Sally Hemings between 1795 and 1808.[30] Jefferson's actions are extremely hypocritical given the fact that he did not view Blacks as equal to whites, regardless of his famous words in the American Declaration of Independence, stating: 'We hold these truths to be self-evident, that all men are created equal.' More importantly, Sally was a product of miscegenation and Jefferson maintained that it was biologically unnatural for whites and Blacks to racially mix![31] Jefferson appears to have overlooked his negative ideas regarding interracial sex on at least five occasions.

In a sense the Jefferson incident exemplifies the taboo and historical denial surrounding miscegenation in the US. Despite the fact that it is woven into the fabric of the society, it is a subject that is largely ignored. Multiracial persons are seen as something 'new' or contemporary rather than as part and parcel of the historical and sociological development of the US. Colour oppression and white supremacy is something inherent to the US and miscegenation is its bogey. The US should come to terms with 'the last big taboo',[32] and admit to the social fact that North Americans are actually more racially mixed than they commonly acknowledge. Denying the history of miscegenation in the US has established further the myths supporting racial distinctions and boundaries.[33]

When the taboo surrounding miscegenation is taken into consideration it is easier to understand why the one drop rule has such potency in US history. Concomitant with this historical amnesia is the way mainstream American historians often fail to acknowledge or appreciate the contribution African Americans have made to US culture. Yet when African American intellectuals challenge the narrow view of Anglo-American history they are accused of 'disuniting America'.[34] At bottom here is a history of social oppression based primarily on 'race' in the US. 'Race-mixing' is an extremely sensitive area to discuss and debate, and many social researchers find it more useful to ignore rather than examine. If miscegenation is discussed it is put in the framework of being a contemporary phenomenon.

A problem with the pressure group calling for a multiracial category in the US (see Chapter 1) is that they fail to fully take into account the significance and fragility of African American numbers. The perspective suggesting that there is a 'new' multiracial group *within* the African American community is both myopic and ahistorical. Especially in view of the fact that between 75 and 90 per cent of African Americans could claim to be of multiracial origins. In examining a multiracial identity, one does not need to have merely a white parent and a Black parent to be considered 'multiracial'. Indeed, many 'pure Blacks' and so-called 'mulattos' in the US married as 'Blacks' in law. But, using a logical reference, these are in effect 'mixed marriages'. It is only in a *socially constructed* sense then that African Americans are 'racially pure'. No doubt there will continue to be heated debate regarding the issue of 'who is Black?' for many years to come in the US.

The UK and the city of Liverpool offer a qualitative perspective on multiracial identity and an understanding of a specific nomenclature. This case is also useful in again indicating how light brown skin does not necessarily mean upward social mobility. In the city of Liverpool there is a relationship between the dynamics of widespread social deprivation and Black disempowerment. With the Black community being in a minority, 'Liverpool-born Blacks' relatively share the same subordinate position as other Black minorities. There is certainly no pattern of social privilege given to the light-skinned over dark-skinned Blacks. However, there does exist an obvious disparity between the rates of employment among the white and Black populaces.[35] Up to 90 per cent of multiracial Black youth in some areas of Liverpool are unemployed, that is three to four times more than the figure for whites.[36] Racialised discrimination has an adverse effect on the life chances of multiracial persons in Liverpool. To assess the extent of it would go beyond the confines of this study, but it is fair to suggest that racial discrimination is an everyday occurrence for many designated 'Liverpool-born Blacks' (see Chapters 2 and 3).

Conclusion

To summarise, during the 1990s much debate took place in 'Black cultural studies' academic circles concerning the issue of 'hybridity' and 'diaspora'. In regard to international multiracial identity each of these concepts has specific relevance. However, the majority of theorists who write extensively on hybridity and diaspora tend to view the concepts in correspondence with ethnicity, migration and the postcolonial experience rather than interraciality.[37] To put it another way, these postmodern theorists tend to view hybridity merely in cultural terms and tend to adopt narrow ahistorical perspectives. Writing within a postcolonial frame of reference, Homi Bhabha states:

> the importance of hybridity is not to be able to trace two original moments from which the third emerges, rather hybridity to me is the 'third space' which enables other positions to emerge. This third space displaces the histories that constitute it, and sets up new structures of authority, new political initiatives, which are inadequately understood through received wisdom.[38]

Hybridity is used by Homi Bhabha primarily in theoretical terms to depict the contemporary 'place' of the ex-colonised in the metropolis. It does not necessarily relate to miscegenation; hybridity is more to do with social, cultural and political syncretism. The 'third space' offers a novel way of understanding the age-worn, almost trite, dichotomies: coloniser/colonised or oppressor/oppressed. Instead, out of these dichotomous histories emerges the 'third space' that is somehow 'free' of its parental and historical lineages. It offers a dynamic, postmodern and anti-imperialist, way to contest the power of the powerful. Although Bhabha's writing is rather turgid, even esoteric at times, it does reveal another way of considering the notion of hybridity, certainly beyond the generally negative usage by British Empire apologists and theorists in relation to human hybridity.[39]

A problem with Bhabha's analysis is in the way he assumes we can simply create something entirely 'new' from two histories. It really is ahistorical in perspective and cannot be deemed logical from the perspective of the life experiences of the once 'colonised' – those persons/groups that have migrated from the satellites to the metropoles. In theory Bhabha may well have touched on something worth considering, but when put to the acid test of the social world it fails. Of course history and culture is dynamic and ever-changing, but the pattern or framework of oppression and social exclusion can often remain a constant. Multiracial persons, for example, cannot simply ignore those histories that created them under the certain sociological dimensions of colonialism. In point of fact more often than not they have had little choice but to side with the 'subordinated history' and social group.

Take the 'coloureds' of South Africa under apartheid: using Bhabha's basic framework, they have emerged primarily via two histories, two peoples – one Black of African descent, one white of European descent – yet it is the connection with their Black/ African heritage which has been the source of their collective oppression. Those 'coloureds' who could find a way to deny their Blackness had a chance to enter the 'white world' of social privilege in South Africa. This was the reality of a 'third space people'. They had little choice in the matter of being 'new' or apart from the histories that produced them. Their social world was interwoven with these 'parent histories'. Taking this into account, it is understandable why Bhabha fails to link his 'hybridity theory' directly to the actual social processes of human interaction and experience at ground level. His analysis is unnecessarily abstract and lacking in ethnographic terms.

In addition, Bhabha fails to accommodate the complexity of these various 'colonial-based histories', as each has specific *internal* hybrid formations that also need to be explained. To view 'Englishness' as a monolithic entity, for example, is not to understand its mongrel origins. Therefore and paradoxically, too many theorists, exemplified by Bhabha, construct rather rigid conceptual frameworks to promote 'fluid theories' of cultural hybridity. But they are bound to be proved wanting when examined in relation to what occurs 'on the ground' in the social world.

The concept of the 'African diaspora' is also gaining recognition within the academy. Professor Stuart Hall has written extensively on this subject and is regarded as a *de facto* guru in Black cultural politics in the UK. He can also be situated in the postmodern school of thought linking the concept of 'diaspora' to hybridity and 'difference' in Black culture. Writing in relation to African Caribbean cinematic themes, Hall maintains:

> The diaspora experience . . . is defined, not by essence or purity, but by the recognition of a necessary heterogeneity and diversity; by a conception of 'identity' which lives with and through, not despite, difference; by *hybridity*. Diaspora identities are those which are constantly producing and reproducing themselves anew, through transformation and difference.[40]

Above, Hall is expressing the 'new' in diasporan experiences. In this sense, for persons of African (Caribbean) descent in the diaspora, it is mythical to try and return to a past, to lost origins. They have long gone, and whether one is located in the Americas, the Caribbean or Europe, having fed into a 'new history' is the 'essence' of one's existence. Looking back to a long-lost African civilisation that is devoid of European hegemony may satisfy in a symbolic sense, but it cannot be recaptured. All, in fact, according to Hall, is renewing itself in cultural terms and is forever provisional.[41]

How is this relevant in the assessment of international multiracial identity? Actually it is rather informative and useful in the sense of describing again the fluidity of identity constructs. Yet what Hall suggests is really not novel in regard to an understanding of the development of the 'New World' and its descendants. For example, as we have already discussed, Jamaicans are essentially a 'hybrid' population. Within this population, however, is a hierarchical colour structure. How does Hall explain this? In fact he does not really consider the implications of this implicit white supremacy. He is more interested in explaining away the syncretism of Black culture itself. There is a celebration of 'hybrid forms', but the issue of social privilege via colour stratification is not considered.[42] Moreover, despite this consolidated effort to prove how Black history and culture is interlocked and fused with African, Caribbean, Asian and European forms, Hall et al. fail to follow the trail of white supremacy to consider just how this has changed form, but remained constant in terms of hegemonic leadership.

In sum, in our assessment of international multiracial identity, it is important to examine the various forms of Black culture and explain the hybrid elements that make it up. Again, to regard this as something 'postmodern' is to be myopic and ahistorical. To be sure it is well documented, even though at times ignored by white supremacists, that world human civilisation is in essence *hybrid*. This may well be a positive way to promote world harmony and understanding of 'race matters'. However, we must not be content with merely celebrating hybridity *per se*; what we also need to know is how humans have socially demarcated themselves – regardless of their similarities and cultural linkages. Multiracial identity, as maintained throughout this study, is a social construct that has special social consequences for certain groups that are defined as such. The experiences do differ around the globe, but there is a common link in the way each multiracial group has interacted with the social forces of white supremacy. Crucially, this chapter has attempted to assess the complexity of a number of international multiracial identities. The following chapter will consider some of the key themes to have emerged from this study.

Conclusion

Multiracial identity is a complex social phenomenon – especially when we consider it from an international point of view. This book offers an introduction to the meandering historical and sociological paths of four global multiracial identity constructs. A number of key themes have emerged that shed light on both the particularity and commonality of multiracial identity experiences. These need to be explored with further empirical research. Certainly in regard to: the development of white supremacy ideology and practice and how it has impacted on and socially engineered 'multiracial groups'; how and why the social structure of a society often determines the way identities are formed; and, given this, the extent to which 'human agency' is relevant to identity construct is important, but how important? These themes need to be examined in far greater detail than that offered here.

However, the UK provided an empirical insight via the views of a long-established Black community, made up of a cohort of multiracial respondents spanning two generations. The fact that the majority of the respondents defined themselves as 'Black British' gives sociological food for thought in assessing a specific multiracial social group. Again, to further existing knowledge, extended empirical research is necessary in order to compare and contrast the views of multiracial respondents from around the world.

It is self-evident, whether it be in the UK, US, South Africa or Jamaica, that the social construction of 'Black identities' is inextricably entwined with the development and growth of white European domination in terms of cultural, political, economic and social determinants. The phrase that encapsulates this domination is more aptly described as 'white supremacy'. This took hold at the outset of the European voyages of discovery into a 'New World' that was already largely inhabited by 'old peoples'. Over centuries of miscegenation, regardless of the various European prohibitions and frequent theoretical disapproval of it, there developed multiracial social groups that were often stigmatised

121

via racialised pseudo-scientific theories espoused by European intellects who advocated Anglo-Saxon cultural and human superiority. Far from being objective, however, many of these European 'intellects' were economically attached to plantation ownership in the 'New World'. In this sense they had much to lose if enslaved peoples of African and Asian heritage were to be openly acknowledged as equal in human status to white Europeans.[1] Indeed it could not be acknowledged that white Europeans were involved in enslaving 'fellow human beings'. On the contrary, it was much more appropriate to categorise them as less than human and fit only for subserviance.

Therefore, in the development of the 'New World' the practice of miscegenation was fostered within unequal power relations between the white European settlers (the colonists) and the indigenous inhabitants (the colonised). The British, according to a nineteenth-century General in the British Army, were a particularly ruthless coloniser.[2] For example, not only did the British take over the land space of a given people on the African continent, they also attempted to annihilate the indigenous cultural identity. And what better way to do this than through the mode of miscegenation?

Even though the practice of interracial mating was taboo, it was still a widespread phenomenon.[3] This study has shown how prevailing and deep-rooted it has been historically in four geographically disparate, yet interlinked, areas. Miscegenation created an incongruous relationship between the coloniser and the colonised. Indeed the very act of interracial sex went against the core European justification for enslaving and colonising African humanity. Yet regardless of the hypocrisy there is ample evidence showing that *desire* for the sexuality of indigenous peoples certainly overcame any preconceived *aversion*, even though mixed unions were often based on force, from rape to concubinage. A number of the 'New World' white slavemasters found it difficult to control human feelings and desire from impinging on the slave/slavemaster relationship.[4] Consequently the outcome of this sexual interaction is seen in the development of multiracial groups wherever white European colonisers settled.

Given the historical legacy of miscegenation in regard to white Europeans and African descended peoples, it is a misnomer to consider it as a contemporary phenomenon – as the current movement for 'multiracial persons' in the US often implies. Without careful consideration of the historical forces that have shaped racialised relations we cannot hope to understand the complex nature of the present situation. Crucially, this study provides a contribution to furthering our understanding of multiracial identities that have been forged in four nations steeped in racialised dominance and oppression. At the dawn of a new millennium, there is still a great need for understanding how inextricably interwoven the human family actually is. All we can state with confidence is this: *all roads lead us back to Africa.*

Notes

Glossary

1 See M. P. P. Root (ed.), *The Multiracial Experience: Racial Borders as the New Frontier* (California: Sage, 1996), p. ix.
2 Ibid., p. x.

1 Multiracial identity in historical context

1 See for example M. Castells, *The Information Age: Economy, Society and Culture, Vol. II: The Power of Identity* (Oxford, UK: Blackwell, 1997); J. Rutherford (ed.), *Identity: Community, Culture, Difference* (London: Lawrence & Wishart, 1990), and J. Donald and A. Rattansi (eds), *'Race', Culture & Difference* (London: Open University and Sage, 1992).
2 There is a growing pressure group in the US led by advocates of 'multiracial identity'. In particular they want the census data to have a racial category designated for 'multiracial persons'. See P. R. Spickard, 'The Illogic of American Racial Categories', in M. P. P. Root (ed.), *Racially Mixed People in America* (California: Sage, 1992), pp. 12–23; M. P. P. Root (ed.), 'A Bill of Rights for Racially Mixed People', in *The Multiracial Experience: Racial Borders as the New Frontier* (California: Sage, 1996), pp. 3–14.
3 C. W. Mills, *The Sociological Imagination* (London: Oxford University Press, 1959), p. 6.
4 D. M. Newman, *Sociology: Exploring the Architecture of Everyday Life*, 2nd ed. (Thousand Oaks, Calif.: Pine Forge Press), p. 120.
5 P. Gilroy, 'Roots and Routes: Black Identity as an Outernational Project', in H. W. Harris, H. C. Blue and E. E. H. Griffith (eds), *Racial and Ethnic Identity: Psychological Development and Creative Expression* (New York and London: Routledge), p. 18.
6 There is a fundamental agreement among the world's major scholars that 'race' is essentially a social construct and has no scientific validity. The United Nations Educational, Scientific and Cultural Organization (UNESCO) produced a series of statements on 'race' confirming this point. See A. Montagu, *Statement on Race: An Annotated Elaboration and Exposition of the Four Statements on Race Issued by the United Nations Educational, Scientific and Cultural Organization, 3rd Edition* (New York: Oxford University Press, 1972). In this regard, S. Small, *The Black Experience in the United States and England in the 1980s* (London and New York: Routledge, 1994), p. 209, writes: 'There are no "races" so there can be no "race relations". When we analyse relations between Blacks and whites we are studying social relations which have been imbued with "racial" meaning.' See also R. Miles, *Racism* (London and New York: Routledge, 1989).
7 See S. Hall, 'Race, Articulation and Societies Structured in Dominance',

in *UNESCO, Sociological Theories: Race and Colonialism* (Paris: UNESCO, 1980).

8   B. Anderson, *Imagined Communities: Reflections on the Origins and Spread of Nationalism* (London: Verso, 1983).

9   S. Hall, 'New Ethnicities', in J. Donald and A. Rattansi (eds), *'Race', Culture & Difference* (London: Open University and Sage, 1992), pp. 252–9.

10   For example, it is difficult to find any of the authors, of whom some are regarded as the 'best' contemporary thinkers in terms of Black culture, such as Stuart Hall and Paul Gilroy, in the following text that are comfortable with the term 'Black'. Yet paradoxically when it comes to selling their collective ideas they appear to have no problem giving the title a distinctly 'Black Identity'. See G. Dent (ed.), *Black Popular Culture* (Seattle: Bay Press, 1992).

11   See Root.

12   J. M. Spencer, *The New Colored People: The Mixed-Race Movement in America* (New York and London: New York University Press, 1997), p. 1.

13   Considering the fact that there is a 25-author contribution in *The Multiracial Experience* text edited by M. P. P. Root, there is not a balance of views. Indeed the text overtly contends for a 'new people' under the term 'multiracial'. In this sense, the historical African American experience of the 'one drop rule' is given cursory attention by only a few of the authors. Even though it has been the determinant factor in what it is to be 'Black in America'; see F. J. Davis, *Who Is Black? One Nation's Definition* (Pennsylvania: Pennsylvania State University Press, 1991).

14   M. K. Asante, 'Racing to Leave the Race: Black Postmodernists Off-Track', *The Black Scholar* 23 (3 and 4; Spring/Fall 1993), pp. 50–1.

15   Ibid., p. 50.

16   F. J. Davis, p. 139.

17   See B. Tizard and A. Phoenix, *Black, White or Mixed Race?: Race and Racism in the Lives of Young People of Mixed Parentage* (London: Routledge, 1993).

18   See R. E. Park, 'Human Migration and the Marginal Man', *The American Journal of Sociology*, 33 (6) (May 1928), pp. 881–93; and 'Mentality of Racial Hybrids', *The American Journal of Sociology*, 36 (Jan. 1931), pp. 534–51.

19   'Human Migration'.

20   Ibid., p. 893.

21   Ibid., p. 881.

22   Ibid.

23   C. Dover, *Half-Caste* (London: Secker & Warburg, 1937), p. 13.

24   Ibid., p. 279.

25   E. V. Stonequist, *Marginal Man: A Study of Personality and Culture Conflict* (New York: Russell & Russell, 1961; first published in 1937).

26   See H. F. Dickie-Clark, 'The Marginal Situation: A Contribution to Marginality Theory', *Social Forces*, 44 (1965), pp. 363–70.

27   Stonequist.

28   Ibid., and R. E. Park.

29   For examples of labelling theory, see H. S. Becker, *Outsiders: Studies in the Sociology of Deviance* (New York: The Free Press, 1973); E. Goffman, *Stigma: Notes on the Management of Spoiled Identity* (Englewood Cliffs,

NJ: Prentice-Hall, 1963); I. Katz, *Stigma: A Social Psychological Analysis* (New Jersey: Lawrence Erlbaum Associates, 1981).

30 J. E. Helms (ed.), *Black and White Racial Identity: Theory, Research and Practice* (London: Praeger, 1993), p. 3.

31 See Tizard and Phoenix, note 17.

32 See M. E. Fletcher, *Report on An Investigation into the Colour Problem in Liverpool and other Ports* (Liverpool, UK: Association for the Welfare of Half-Caste Children, 1930).

33 L. Wirth and H. Goldhamer, 'The Hybrid and the Problem of Miscegenation', in O. Klineberg (ed.), *Characteristics of the American Negro* (New York: Harper & Row, 1944), part V; and G. Myrdal, *An American Dilemma*, vols. I and II (New York: Harper & Row, 1944).

34 Wirth and Goldhamer, p. 340.

35 F. J. Davis, pp. 8–11.

36 Ibid., p. 9.

37 Wirth and Goldhamer, p. 369.

38 See for example K. Russell, M. Wilson and R. Hall, *The Color Complex: The Politics of Skin Color Among African Americans* (New York: Harcourt Brace Jovanovich, 1992), who analyse the issue of 'skin tone' within the African American experience and argue that it has and still does have great significance within the community.

39 P. R. Spickard, 'The Illogic of American Racial Categories', in Root (ed.), *Racially Mixed People in America*, p. 21.

40 See for example G. R. Daniel, 'Beyond Black and White: The New Multiracial Consciousness', in Root (ed.), *Racially Mixed People in America*, pp. 121–39; M. C. Thornton, 'Hidden Agendas, Identity Theories, and Multiracial People', in Root, (ed.) *The Multiracial Experience*, pp. 101–20. These writers exemplify the core arguments of the multiracial pressure group in the US, who are advocating for the 2000 census to have a 'multiracial' category.

41 Spickard, p. 385.

42 Root (ed.), *Racially Mixed People in America*, p. 181.

43 Ibid., p. 182.

44 Reported as a front-page headline in *USA Today* (30 Oct. 1997).

45 Ibid.

46 C. C. I. Hall, '2001: A Race Odyssey', in Root (ed.), *The Multiracial Experience*, p. 409.

47 Professor William Strickland, cited by M. K. Frisby, 'Black, White or Other', in *Emerge* (Dec./Jan., 1996), pp. 48–52.

48 See W. D. Jordan, *White Over Black: American Attitudes Toward the Negro, 1550–1812* (Baltimore, MD: Penguin, 1969), p. 163.

49 For example, see A. Wilson, *Mixed Race Children: A Study of Identity* (London: Allen & Unwin, 1987), pp. 38–63. Wilson is a UK scholar and her discussion in chapter 3 relates to the 'Doll Studies' conducted by the US scholars K. B. Clark and M. K. Clark, 'The Development of Consciousness of Self and the Emergence of Racial Identification in Negro Pre-School Children', in *Journal of Social Psychology*, SSPSI Bulletin 10 (1939), pp. 591–9; see also by the same authors 'Racial Identification and Preference in Negro Children', in T. Newcomb and E. Hartley (eds), *Readings in Social Psychology* (New York: Holt, Rinehart and Winston, 1947), pp. 169–78.

50 R. Moore, *Ethnic Statistics and the 1991 Census – the Black Population of Inner Liverpool* (London: Runneymede, 1994), p. 9.

51 See Y. Alibhai-Brown and A. Montague, *The Colour of Love: Mixed Race Relationships* (London: Virago, 1992); C. Bagley, 'Interracial Marriage in Britain: Some Statistics', in *New Community* 1 (4) (1972), pp. 318–26; S. Benson, *Ambiguous Ethnicity: Interracial Families in London* (Cambridge: Cambridge University Press, 1981); and B. Day, *Sexual Life Between Blacks and Whites* (London: Collins, 1974).

52 See Wilson, note 49, and Tizard and Phoenix, note 17.

53 Ibid.

54 Table adapted from Commission for Racial Equality's, *Roots for the Future: Ethnic Diversity in the Making of Britain* (London: CRE, 1996), p. 38.

55 Wilson, p. vi.

56 Ibid., p. vii.

57 Ibid.

58 Tizard and Phoenix, p. 161.

59 See R. Miles and A. Phizacklea, *White Man's Country: Racism in British Politics* (London: Pluto, 1984).

60 See for example A. Gill, *Ruling Passions: Sex, Race and Empire* (London: BBC Books, 1995); R. May and R. Cohen, 'Interaction Between Race and Colonialism: A Case Study of the Race Riots of 1919 Liverpool', in *Race and Class* 16 (2) (1974), pp. 111–26; P. B. Rich, *Race and Empire in British Politics* (Cambridge: Cambridge University Press, 1986); R. J. C. Young, *Colonial Desire: Hybridity in Theory, Culture and Race* (London: Routledge, 1995).

61 See L. Poliakov, *The Aryan Myth* (London: Chatto, 1974).

62 J. Small, 'Transracial Placements: Conflicts and Contradictions', in S. Ahmed, J. Cheetham and J. Small (eds), *Social Work with Black Children and their Families* (London: Batsford, 1986), pp. 81–99.

63 See M. Macey. '"Same Race" Adoption Policy: Anti-Racism or Racism?', in *Journal of Social Policy* 24 (4), pp. 437–91; also Tizard and Phoenix, note 31, and Wilson, note 49.

64 J. Small, pp. 91–2.

65 Ibid.

66 N. Banks, 'Mixed-Up Kid', in *Social Work Today* (10 Sept. 1992), pp. 12–13.

67 See Tizard and Phoenix, note 17, and Wilson, note 49.

2 Speaking for themselves (I): Definitions of the racial self and parental influence

1 See P. Parmar, 'Black Feminism: The Politics of Articulation', in J. Rutherford (ed.), *Identity: Community, Culture, Difference* (London: Lawrence & Wishart, 1990), pp. 101–26.

2 See M. Christian, 'Black Struggle for Historical Recognition in Liverpool', in *North West Labour History* (20) (1995/6), pp. 58–66; and 'An African-Centered Approach to the Black British Experience: With Special Reference to Liverpool', in *Journal of Black Studies* 28 (3) (Jan. 1998), pp. 291–308; I. Law and J. Henfrey, *A History of Race and Racism in*

Liverpool: 1660–1950 (Liverpool: Merseyside Community Relations Council, 1981).

3 A. M. Gifford, W. Brown and R. Bundey, *Loosen the Shackles: First Report of the Liverpool 8 Enquiry into Race Relations in Liverpool* (London: Karia Press, 1989).

4 G. Ben-Tovim, 'Race Politics and Urban Regeneration: Lessons from Liverpool', in M. Parkinson, B. Foley and D. Judd (eds), *Regenerating the Cities* (Manchester, UK: Manchester University Press, 1988), pp. 141–55.

5 See M. Connelly, K. Roberts, G. Ben-Tovim and P. Torkington, *Black Youth in Liverpool* (The Netherlands: Giordano Culemborg, 1992).

6 See Parmar, note 1, pp. 101–26.

7 S. Hall, 'New Ethnicities', in J. Donald and A. Rattansi (eds), *'Race', Culture & Difference* (London: Sage & Open University Press, 1992), pp. 252–9.

8 W. E. B. Du Bois, *The Souls of Black Folk* (Canada: New American Library, 1982; first published in 1903).

9 See references in note 2.

10 For example, R. E. Park, 'Human Migration and the Marginal Man', in *The American Journal of Sociology* 33 (6) (1928), p. 881, suggests the 'mixed blood' lives a life of inner conflict and psychological malaise in which she is estranged from both the 'Black and white' worlds.

11 Parmar, note 1.

3 Speaking for themselves (II): Inside and outside of blackness in Liverpool, UK

1 I thank Tina Tamsho, a UK poet, for allowing me to use her poem, copyright 1993.

2 See M. Sherwood, *Pastor Daniels Ekarte and the African Churches Mission* (London: Savannah Press, 1994), pp. 118–21.

3 See M. Christian, 'Black Struggle for Historical Recognition in Liverpool', in *North West Labour History* (20) (1995/6), pp. 58–66; and S. Small, 'Racialised Relations in Liverpool: A Contemporary Anomaly', in *New Community* 17 (4) (1991), pp. 511–37.

4 T. Morrison, *The Bluest Eye* (London: Picador, 1990; first published in 1970).

4 South Africa and Jamaica: 'Other' multiracial case studies

1 C. Wright Mills, *The Sociological Imagination* (London: Oxford University Press, 1959), p. 143.

2 P. L. van den Berghe, *Race and Racism: A Comparative Perspective*, 2nd edn (New York: John Wiley & Sons, 1978), p. 96.

3 Ibid., pp. 96–7.

4 Ibid., p. 97.

5 Ibid., p. 98.

6 See *The Hutchinson Concise Encyclopaedia* (Oxford: Helicon, 1994), p. 862.

7　M. Benson, *Nelson Mandela* (Harmondsworth: Penguin, 1986), p. 35.
8　N. Mandela, *Long Walk to Freedom: The Autobiography of Nelson Mandela* (London: Little Brown, 1994), p. 104.
9　Ibid., p. 106.
10　Reported in the *Independent* (7 Feb. 1997), p. 10.
11　Van den Berghe, note 2, p. 107.
12　G. M. Fredrickson, *White Supremacy: A Comparative Study in American & South African History* (Oxford: Oxford University Press, 1981), p. 133.
13　Ibid.
14　Ibid., p. 135.
15　There is need for more empirical research into how the various South African 'races' are progressing within the New South Africa.
16　See *The Hutchinson Concise Encyclopaedia*, p. 494.
17　H. Hoetink, '"Race" and Color in the Caribbean', in S. W. Mintz and S. Price (eds), *Caribbean Contours* (Baltimore: John Hopkins University Press, 1985), p. 69.
18　Ibid.
19　Confirmed in an interview with Professor Barry Chevannes, Dean of Social Sciences, at the University of West Indies, Mona, Jamaica, 4 June 1998.
20　W. Rodney, *The Groundings with my Brothers* (London: Bogle-L'Overture, 1975), p. 16.
21　Ibid.
22　L. Spencer-Strachan, *Confronting the Color Crisis in the African Diaspora: Emphasis Jamaica* (New York: African World Infosystems, 1992), p. 17.
23　See also E. Braithwaite, *The Development of Creole Society in Jamaica: 1770–1820* (Oxford: Clarendon Press, 1971); M. Kerr, *Personality and Conflict in Jamaica* (Liverpool: University of Liverpool Press, 1952).
24　A. Trollope, *The West Indies and the Spanish Main* (New York: Hippocrene, 1985; first published in 1859), pp. 56–7.
25　See Spencer-Strachan, note 22.
26　For a discussion relating to the British empire and its concomitant racial theories, see S. K. Yeboah, *The Ideology of Racism* (London: Hansib, 1988); and P. B. Rich, *Prospero's Return?: Historical Essays on Race, Culture and British Society* (London: Hansib, 1994), chs 1, 2, 4 and 5.
27　Spencer-Strachan, note 22, p. 43.
28　See P. L. van de Berghe, *South Africa: A Study of Conflict* (Berkeley, Calif.: University of California Press, 1967); and I. Goldin, *Making Race: The Politics and Economics of Coloured Identity in South Africa* (London: Longman, 1987).
29　See for example L. Funeburg, *Black, White, Other: Biracial Americans Talk About Race and Identity* (New York: Quill, 1994). This qualitative study relates to the US experience of 42 adult multiracial persons. Yet it fails to give a historical account of how 'race' in the US was socially engineered via enslavement, colonialism, segregation and second-class citizenship for 'people of colour'. Instead it merely examines the views of the respondents in a contemporary sense, a major flaw in the analysis.
30　See Mills, note 1.
31　Interview with Professor Barry Chevannes, Dean of Social Sciences, at the University of West Indies, Mona, Jamaica, 4 June 1998. See also B. Chevannes, *Rastafari: Roots and Ideology* (New York: Syracuse University Press, 1995).

32 For a classic disscussion relating to the social consequences of 'label-ling' and how the process often has consequences that trap the individual into a particular social identity, see H. S. Becker, *Outsiders: Studies in the Sociology of Deviance* (New York: Free Press, 1973).

5 Assessing multiracial identity

1 J. O. Ifekwunigwe, 'Diaspora's Daughters, Africa's Orphans? On Lineage, Authenticity and "Mixed Race" Identity', in H. S. Mirza (ed.), *Black British Feminism: A Reader* (London: Routledge, 1997), p. 146.
2 Ibid.
3 See P. Fryer, *Staying Power: The History of Black People in Britain* (London: Pluto, 1984), ch. 7.
4 For example, in relation to the occupation of Tasmania by the British in the eighteenth and nineteenth centuries and the genocide of the indigenous population, Fryer writes in *Black People in the British Empire: An Introduction* (London: Pluto Press, 1988), p. 38: 'For 30 years black Tasmanians were pitilessly hunted down, tortured and put to death. Men and boys were castrated and otherwise mutilated; women were raped, flogged and burnt with brands; children's brains were dashed out. Some black Tasmanians were tied to trees and used as targets for shooting practice. One old woman was roasted alive. Another woman had her dead husband's head hung round her neck and was driven in front of her captor as his prize. One settler kept a pickle-tub into which he tossed the ears of the black people he shot.'
5 Ibid., pp. 66–72.
6 G. M. Fredrickson, *White Supremacy: A Comparative Study in American & South African History* (Oxford: Oxford Unversity Press, 1981), p. xi.
7 One scholar largely overlooked in the analysis of miscegenation is J. A. Rogers (1880–1966). He was a self-educated man and a prolific writer who, among other works, contributed three volumes covering the sub-ject of miscegenation. He provides profound evidence relating to the contradictions of white supremacist thought and practice. Rogers stated in the 1952 edition, and Foreword, of volume I: 'Racial doctrines as they exist today negate intelligence.' See J. A. Rogers, *Sex and Race*, vols I, II, III (New York: Helga M. Rogers, 1968; first published in 1942 and 1944).
8 C. W. Mills, *The Racial Contract* (Ithaca: Cornell University Press, 1997), p. 1. For another detailed critique of white supremacy in relation to European philosophy see M. Ani, *Yurugu: An African-Centered Critique of European Cultural Thought and Behavior* (Trenton, NJ: African World Press, 1994).
9 Mills, note 8, p. 4.
10 See for example M. P. P. Root (ed.), *Racially Mixed People in America* (California: Sage, 1992); and *The Multiracial Experience: Racial Borders as the New Frontier* (California: Sage, 1996). These collaborative works are ahistorical in terms of the analysis of multiracial identities, particularly in the US context.
11 M. Thatcher, *Britain and Europe* (London: Conservative Political Centre, 1988), p. 2.

12 Many of the authors discussed in Chapter 1 imply that mulitracial persons are a type of 'new people', but this is an erroneous and half-baked perspective that is devoid of the manifold historical evidence pointing to the contrary.

13 F. J. Davis, *Who Is Black?: One Nation's Definition* (Pennsylvania: Pennsylvania State University Press, 1991), p. 82.

14 Ibid., p. 83.

15 Ibid.

16 Ibid., p. 87.

17 Ibid., p. 89.

18 Confirmed by Professor Barry Chevannes, Dean of the Social Sciences, at Mona, Jamaica, University of West Indies, in an interview (4 June 1998).

19 Davis, note 13, p. 109.

20 Ibid., p. 110.

21 For example, in the US there were elite 'mulatto' cliques, especially in Louisiana, and the main criterion for membership was light skin tone. Another way of membership was through the 'brown paper bag test'. If 'Blacks' were darker than a brown paper bag they would not be admitted into the 'blue vein societies'. See J. Williamson, *New People: Miscegenation and Mulattoes in the United States* (New York: New York University Press, 1984); also, J. W. Johnson, *The Autobiography of an Ex-Colored Man* (New York: Dover Publications, 1995; first published in 1912).

22 Davis, note 13, p. 117.

23 Ibid.

24 J. O. Ifekwunigwe, note 1, p. 147.

25 I have argued this point in relation to the UK and US elsewhere, see M. Christian, 'An African-Centered Approach to the Black British Experience: with Special Reference to Liverpool', *Journal of Black Studies* 28 (3) (Jan. 1998), pp. 291–308.

26 See D. Weekes, 'Shades of Blackness: Young Black Female Constructions of Beauty', in H. S. Mirza (ed.), *Black British Feminism: A Reader* (London: Routledge, 1997), pp. 113–26.

27 The relative upward mobility of dark-skinned Jamaicans was confirmed to me in an interview with Professor Barry Chevannes, Dean of Social Sciences, University of West Indies, at Mona, Jamaica, 4 June 1998. He did state, however, that Jamaica is still very much an unequal society based on both class and skin-tone privileges.

28 See W. D. Jordan, *White over Black: American Attitudes Toward the Negro 1550–1812* (Baltimore, Md.: Pelican, 1969).

29 See Davis, note 13; and K. Russell, M. Wilson and R. Hall, *The Color Complex: the Politics of Skin Color Among African Americans* (New York: Harcourt Brace Jovanovich, 1992).

30 Jordan, note 28, pp. 464–9.

31 Thomas Jefferson's views on white supremacy over Black peoples are cited in W. Dudley (ed.), *African Americans: Opposing Viewpoints* (San Diego, Calif.: Greenhaven Press, 1997), pp. 23–9.

32 As suggested in Davis, note 13, p. 171.

33 See E. Gable, 'Maintaining Boundaries, or "Mainstreaming" Black History in a White Museum', in S. Macdonald and G. Fyfe (eds), *Theorizing Museums* (Oxford: Blackwell, 1996), pp. 177–202.

34 See A. M. Schlesinger, Jr., *The Disuniting of America: Reflections on a Multiracial Society* (New York: W. W. Norton, 1992).

35 See A. M. Gifford, W. Brown and R. Bundey, *Loosen the Shackles: First Report of the Liverpool 8 Inquiry into Race Relations in Liverpool* (London: Karia Press, 1989).

36 Information on the contemporary national trend for Black unemployment in the UK can be sought from: 'Race for the Election', c/o Churches Commission for Racial Justice, Inter Church House, 35 Lower Marsh, London SE1 7RL, UK.

37 See H. K. Bhabha (ed.), *Nation and Narration* (London: Routledge, 1990); his *The Location of Culture* (London: Routledge, 1994); and 'The Third Space', in J. Rutherford (ed.), *Identity, Culture, Community Difference* (London: Lawrence & Wishart, 1990), pp. 207–21; P. Gilroy, *The Black Atlantic: Modernity and Double Consciousness* (London: Verso, 1993); S. Hall, 'Cultural Identity and Diaspora', in J. Rutherford (ed.), *Identity, Culture, Community Difference* (London: Lawrence & Wishart, 1990), pp. 222–37.

38 H. Bhabha, 'The Third Space', p. 221.

39 See R. J. C. Young, *Colonial Desire: Hybridity in Theory, Culture and Race* (London: Routledge, 1995), pp. 6–12.

40 Hall, note 37, p. 235.

41 Ibid., p. 236.

42 Ibid.

Conclusion

1 For example, Edward Long and Bryan Edwards are two eighteenth-century white historians and plantation owners who wrote extensively about the inferiority of Black people in the Caribbean. Both were bestselling authors and commanded major influence via their works. For a detailed analysis of these writers and the impact they had on racist ideology, see J. Walvin, *The Black Presence: a Documentary History of the Negro in England: 1555–1860* (London: Orbach & Chambers, 1971).

2 British General Sir Thomas Monroe stated in 1818: 'Foreign conquerors have treated the natives with violence, and often with great cruelty, but none has treated them with so much scorn as we'; cited in A. Gill, *Ruling Passions: Sex, Race and Empire* (London: BBC, 1995), p. 20.

3 Ibid.

4 As mentioned above, a case in point involves the third President of the US, Thomas Jefferson, who had a long relationship with his African American slave, Sally Hemings, who is rumoured to have borne him five children. See note 28, ch. 5.

Bibliography

Abarry, A. S. 'Afrocentricity' in *Journal of Black Studies* 21 (2) (1990), pp. 123–5.

Ackah, W. and Christian, M. (eds) *Black Organisation and Identity in Liverpool: A Local, National and Global Perspective* (Liverpool: Charles Wootton College, 1997).

Adi, H. *African and Caribbean Communities in Britain* (East Sussex: Wayland, 1995).

Akbar, N. *The Community of Self* (Tallahassee, Fla.: Mind Productions & Associates, 1985).

Akbar, N. *Visions for Black Men* (Nashville, Tenn.: Winston-Derek, 1991).

Alibhai-Brown, Y. and Montague, A. *The Colour of Love: Mixed Race Relationships* (London: Virago, 1992).

Alibhai-Brown, Y. 'Black Looks White Lies', *Guardian* (7 Dec. 1996).

Allen, S. 'The Institutionalization of Racism' in *Race* 15 (1) (1973), pp. 99–106.

Anderson, B. *Imagined Communities: Reflections on the Origins and Spread of Nationalism* (London: Verso, 1983).

Anderson, D. G. *Nigger Lover* (London: Fowler, undated).

Asante, M. K. and Abdulai S. V. (eds) *Contemporary Black Thought: Alternative Analyses in Social and Behavioral Science* (London: Sage, 1980).

Asante, M. K. *The Afrocentric Idea* (Philadelphia: Temple University Press, 1998, rev. edn).

Asante, M. K. *Afrocentricity* (Trenton, NJ: Africa World Press, 1988).

Asante, M. K. *Kemet, Afrocentricity and Knowledge* (Trenton, NJ: African World Press, 1990).

Asante, M. K. *Malcolm X as Cultural Hero & Other Afrocentric Essays* (Trenton, NJ: Africa World Press, 1993).

Asante, M. K. 'Racing to Leave the Race: Black Postmodernists Off-Track', *The Black Scholar*, 23 (3 and 4) (1993).

Asante, M. K. 'Afrocentricity, Race, and Reason', *Race & Reason* (Autumn 1994), pp. 20–2.

Asante, M. K. 'Are You Scared of Your Shadow?: A Critique of Sidney Lemelle's "The Politics of Cultural Existence"' in *Journal of Black Studies* 26 (4) (1996), pp. 524–33.

Aughton, P. *Liverpool: A People's History* (Preston: Carnegie, 1993).

Bagley, C. 'Patterns of Inter-Ethnic Marriage in Great Britain', *Phylon* 33 (1972), pp. 373–9.

Bagley, C. 'Interracial Marriage in Britain: Some Statistics', *New Community* 1 (4) (1972), pp. 318–26.

Bagley, C. 'Inter-Ethnic Marriage in Britain and the United States from 1970–1977: A Selected Bibliography' in *Sage Race Relations Abstracts* 4 (1) (1979).

Bagley, C. 'Mixed Marriages and Race Relations Today' in *Patterns of Prejudice* 15 (1) (1981), pp. 33–44.

Baker, H. A., Diawara, M. and Lindeborg, R. H. (eds) *Black British Cultural Studies* (Chicago: Chicago University Press, 1996).

Banks, N. 'Mixed-Up Kid' in *Social Work Today* (10 Sept. 1992), pp. 12–13.

Bannerman, H. *The Story of Little Black Sambo* (London: Chatto & Windus, 1899).

Bannerman, H. *The Story of Sambo and the Twins: A New Adventure of Little Black Sambo* (London: Nisbet, 1937).

Banton, M. *The Coloured Quarter: Negro Immigrants in an English City* (London: Cape, 1955).

Banton, M. *White and Coloured: The Behaviour of British People Towards Coloured Immigrants* (London: Cape, 1959).

Banton, M. 'Social Distance: A New Appreciation' in *The Sociological Review* (Dec. 1960), pp. 169–83.

Banton, M. and Harwood, J. *The Race Concept* (Newton Abbot: David and Charles, 1975).

Banton, M. *The Idea of Race* (London: Tavistock, 1977).

Banton, M. 'Analytical and Folk Concepts of Race and Ethnicity' in *Ethnic and Racial Studies* 2 (2) (1979), pp. 127–38.

Banton, M. *Racial Consciousness* (London: Longman, 1988).

Barker, M. *The New Racism: Conservatives and the Ideology of the Tribe* (London: Hutchinson, 1981).

Barrow, W. M. *Studies in the History of Liverpool: 1756–1783* (Unpublished MA thesis: University of Liverpool, 1925).

Barth, F. *Ethnic Groups and Boundaries: The Social Organization of Culture Difference* (London: George Allen & Unwin, 1969).

Baxter, P. and Sansom, B. (eds) *Race and Social Difference* (Harmondsworth: Penguin, 1972).

Becker, H. S. 'Whose Side Are We On?' in *Social Problems* 14 (Winter 1967), pp. 239–47.

Becker, H. S. *Outsiders: Studies in The Sociology of Deviance* (New York: The Free Press, 1973).

Bell, D. *Faces at the Bottom of the Well: The Permanence of Racism* (New York: Basic Books, 1992).

Benson, M. *Nelson Mandela* (Harmondsworth: Penguin, 1986).

Benson, S. *Ambiguous Ethnicity: Interracial Families in London* (Cambridge: Cambridge University Press, 1981).

Ben-Tovim, G. (ed.), *Equal Opportunities and the Employment of Black People and Ethnic Minorities on Merseyside: A Report of a Conference Plus Resource Materials* (Liverpool: Mersey Area Profile Group, 1983).

Ben-Tovim, G., Gabriel, J., Law, I. and Stredder, K. *Local Politics of Race* (Basingstoke: Macmillan, 1986).

Bhabha, H. K. (1990) 'The Third Space: Interview with Homi Bhabha' in J. Rutherford (ed.), *Identity: Community, Culture, Difference* (London: Lawrence & Wishart, 1990), pp. 207–21.

Bhabha, H. K. *The Location of Culture* (London: Routledge, 1994).

Bhabha, H. K. 'The Other Question: Difference, Discrimination, and the Discourse of Colonialism' in H. A. Baker, Jr., M. Diawara and R. H. Lindeborg (eds), *Black British Cultural Studies: A Reader* (Chicago: Chicago University Press, 1996), pp. 87–113.

Bhat, A., Car-Hill, R. and Ohri, S. (eds) *Britain's Black Population: A New Perspective*, 2nd edn (Aldershot: Gower, 1988).

Blauner, R. *Racial Oppression in America* (New York: Harper & Row, 1972).

Bloom, L. *The Social Psychology of Race Relations* (London: George Allen & Unwin, 1971).

Boggs, J. *Racism and Class Struggle: Further Pages from a Black Worker's Note-book* (New York: Monthly Review Press, 1970).

Bogle, D. *Toms, Coons, Mulattoes, Mamies and Bucks: An Interpretive History of Blacks in American Films* (New York: Continuum, 1992).

Bolt, C. *Victorian Attitudes to Race* (London: Routledge & Kegan Paul, 1971).

Bose, M. 'One Corner . . . is Forever England' in *New Society* 47 (848) (1979), pp. 7–9.

Bourne, J. 'Cheerleaders and Ombudsmen: The Sociology of Race Relations in Britain' in *Race & Class* 21 (4) (1980), pp. 331–52.

Braithwaite, E. *The Development of Creole Society in Jamaica: 1770–1820* (Oxford: Clarendon, 1971).

Brogden, M. and Brogden, A. 'From Henry III to Liverpool 8: The Unity of Police Street Powers' in *International Journal of the Sociology of Law* 12 (1984), pp. 37–58.

Brogden, M. *On the Mersey Beat: Policing Liverpool between the Wars* (Oxford: Oxford University Press, 1991).

Brown, M. *Image of a Man: A Primer on what a Black Man is and on How to be a Black Man* (New York: East Publications, 1976).

Brown, M. K. *They Haven't Done Nothing Yet: L8* (Liverpool: Race & Social Policy Unit, University of Liverpool, 1993).

Brown, W. *How Liverpool has Underdeveloped its Blacks* (Unpublished paper: Manchester Polytechnic, 1979).

Brown, W. *Race, Class and Educational Inequality: A Case Study of Liverpool Born Blacks* (Unpublished MA thesis: University of Liverpool, 1986).

Bryan, P. *The Jamaican People, 1880–1902: Race, Class and Social Control* (London: Macmillan, 1991).

Burns, A. *Colour Prejudice: With Particular Reference to the Relationship between Whites and Negroes* (London: George Allan & Unwin, 1948).

Callinicos, A. *Race and Class* (London: Bookmarks, 1993).

Cameron, G. and Crooke, S. *Liverpool: Capital of the Slave Trade* (Liverpool: Liverpool City Council, 1992).

Camper, C. (ed.), *Miscegenation Blues: Voices of Mixed Race Women* (Canada: Sister Vision, 1994).

Caradog-Jones, D. *The Economic Status of Coloured Families in the Port of Liverpool* (Liverpool: Liverpool University Press, 1940).

Carey, A. T. *Colonial Students: A Study of the Social Adaptation of Colonial Students in London* (London: Secker and Warburg, 1956).

Carlyle, T. 'The Nigger Question', in *Critical and Miscellaneous Essays: vol. VII* (London: Chapman and Hall, 1849).

Centre for Contemporary Cultural Studies. *The Empire Strikes Back: Race and Racism in 1970s Britain* (London: Hutchinson, 1982).

Cesaire, A. *Discourse on Colonialism* (New York: Monthly Review Press, 1972; first published 1955).

Chandler, G. *An Illustrated History of Liverpool* (Liverpool: Rondo, 1972).

Charles Wootton Students. *Speaking for Ourselves: Poems from the Charles Wootton Centre* (Liverpool: Charles Wootton Press, 1981).

Chevannes, B. *Rastafari: Roots and Ideology* (New York: Syracuse University Press, 1995).

Christian, M. 'Black Struggle for Historical Recognition in Liverpool' in *North West Labour History* 20 (1995), pp. 58–66.

Christian, M. 'The Black Community in Liverpool: Current Perspectives and

Issues' in *Charles Wootton News* (Liverpool: Charles Wootton College Press, 1995).

Christian, M. 'An African-Centred Approach to the Black British Experience: With Special Reference to Liverpool' in *Journal of Black Studies* 28 (3) (1998), pp. 291–308.

Christian, M. 'Empowerment and Black Communities in the UK: With Special Reference to Liverpool' in *Community Development Journal* 33 (1) (1998), pp. 18–31.

Clark, K. B. and Clark, M. K. (1939) 'The Development of Consciousness of Self and the Emergence of Racial Identification in Negro Pre-School Children' in *Journal of Social Psychology*, SSPSI Bulletin 10 (1939), pp. 591–9.

Clark, K. B. and Clark, M. K. 'Racial Identification and Preference in Negro Children' in T. Newcomb and E. Hartley (eds), *Readings in Social Psychology* (New York: Holt, Rinehart and Winston, 1947), pp. 169–78.

Clark, K. B. *Dark Ghetto: Dilemmas of Social Power* (New York: Harper & Row, 1967).

Clay, D. *10 Years On: 1981–1991, Looking Back Over the Years* (Unpublished paper, 1991).

Collins, P. H. *Black Feminist Thought: Knowledge, Consciousness, and the Politics of Empowerment* (New York: Routledge, 1991).

Collins, S. 'The Social Position of White and "Half-Caste" Women in Colored Groupings in Britain' in *American Sociological Review* 16 (6) (1951), pp. 796–802.

Collins, S. 'The British-Born Coloured' in *Sociological Review* 3 (1) (1955), pp. 77–92.

Collins, S. *Coloured Minorities in Britain* (London: Lutterworth, 1957).

Coleman, D. 'Ethnic Intermarriage in Great Britain' in *Population Trends* (40) (1985), pp. 4–10.

Commission for Racial Equality. *Five Views of Multi-Racial Britain* (London: CRE, 1978).

Commission for Racial Equality. *Roots of the Future: Ethnic Diversity in the Making of Britain* (London: CRE, 1996).

Conference Report on Race Relations in Liverpool. *The Question of Colour in Liverpool*, Liverpool, 15–16 Nov. at Holy Lodge High School (Unpublished paper, 1957).

Connelly, M., Roberts, K., Ben-Tovim, G., Torkington, P. T. *Black Youth in Liverpool* (Netherlands: Giordano Bruno Culemborg, 1992).

Connerton, P. (ed.), *Critical Sociology* (Harmondsworth: Penguin, 1976).

Cooper, A. J. *A Voice from the South* (New York: Oxford University Press, 1988, first published in 1892).

Cooper, P. 'Competing Explanations of the Merseyside Riots 1981' in *British Journal of Criminology* 25 (1) (1985), pp. 60–9.

Costello, R. H. *British Attitudes to the Education of Black People with Special Reference to Liverpool's Afro-Caribbean Community 1763–1939* (Unpublished MA thesis: University of Liverpool, 1988).

Costello, R. H. *The Psychosocial History of Black People of the Diaspora as a Factor in the Underachievement of British Pupils of Afro-Caribbean Descent* (Unpublished Ph.D. thesis: University of Liverpool, 1992).

CRE and BBC. *Race Through the 1990s* (London: CRE and BBC, 1992).

Crow, G. 'The Use of the Concept of "Strategy" in Recent Sociological Literature' in *Sociology* 23 (1) (1989), pp. 1–24.

Cross, W. E. *Shades of Blackness: Diversity in African-American Identity* (Philadelphia: Temple University Press, 1991).

Cross, W. E. 'In Search of Blackness and Afrocentricity: The Psychology of Black Identity Change' in H. W. Harris, H. C. Blue and E. E. H. Griffith (eds), *Racial and Ethnic Identity: Psychological Development and Creative Expression* (New York: Routledge, 1995), pp. 53–72.

Curtis, L. P. *Anglo-Saxons and Celts: A Study of Anti-Irish Prejudice in Victorian England* (Connecticut: University of Bridgeport, 1968).

Dabydeen, D. *The Black Presence in English Literature* (Manchester: Manchester University Press, 1985).

Daniel, G. R. 'Beyond Black and White: The New Multiracial Consciousness' in M. P. P. Root (ed.), *Racially Mixed People in America* (London: Sage, 1992), pp. 333–41.

Daniel, G. R. 'Black and White Identity in the New Millennium: Unsevering the Ties That Bind', in M. P. P. Root (ed.), *The Multiracial Experience: Racial Borders as the New Frontier* (London: Sage, 1996), pp. 121–39.

Davison, R. B. *West Indian Migrants: Social and Economic Facts of Migration from the West Indies* (London: Oxford University Press for Institute of Race Relations, 1962).

Day, B. *Sexual Life Between Blacks and Whites* (London: Collins, 1974).

Degler, C. N. *Neither Black Nor White: Slavery and Race Relations in Brazil and the United States* (New York: Macmillan, 1971).

Dickens, C. *The Uncommercial Traveller and Reprinted Pieces* (Oxford: Oxford University Press, 1981; first published in 1861).

Dickie-Clark, H. F. (1966) 'The Marginal Situation: A Contribution to Marginality Theory' in *Social Forces* 44 (1966), pp. 363–70.

'Dicky Sam'. *Liverpool and Slavery: An Historical Account of the Liverpool-African Slave Trade* (Liverpool: Scouse Press, 1984; first published in 1884).

Dimbleby, J. 'Black and White in Liverpool 8' in *New Statesman*, (25 Aug. 1972), pp. 250–52.

Dingwall, E. J. *Racial Pride and Prejudice* (London: Watts & Co, 1946).

Donald, J. and Rattansi, A. (eds) *'Race', Culture & Difference* (London: Sage, 1992).

Dover, C. *Half-Caste* (London: Secker & Warburg, 1937).

Dover, C. *Hell in the Sunshine* (London: Secker & Warburg, 1943).

Drake, St. C. and Cayton, H. *Black Metropolis: A Study of Negro Life in a Northern City, vols. 1 and 2* (New York: Harper & Row, 1962).

Drake, St. C. 'The "Colour Problem" in Britain: A Study of in Social Definitions' in *Sociological Review* 3 (2) (1955), pp. 197–217.

Du Bois, W. E. B. *The Souls of Black Folk* (Canada: New American Library, 1982; first published in 1903).

Du Bois, W. E. B. *The Negro* (London: Oxford University Press, 1970; first published in 1915).

Early Years Trainers Anti-Racist Network. *The Best of Both Worlds: Celebrating Mixed Parentage* (London: EYTARN, 1995).

Early Years Trainers Anti-Racist Network. *Conference Report: Mixed Parentage, Exploring the Issues* (London: EYTARN, 1996).

Edwards, J. 'Why Black Men Date White Women' in *Pride* (June/July 1996), pp. 40–5.

Eidheim, H. 'When Ethnic Identity is a Social Stigma' in F. Barth (ed.), *Ethnic Groups and Social Boundaries: The Social Organization of Culture Difference* (London: George Allen & Unwin, 1969).

Eriksen, T. H. *Ethnicity and Nationalism: Anthropological Perspectives* (London: Pluto, 1993).

Fanon, F. *Black Skin, White Masks* (London: Pluto, 1986; first published in 1952).

Fenton, S. '"Race Relations" in the Sociological Enterprise (A Review Article)' in *New Community* 8 (1/2) (1980), pp. 162–8.

Fenton, S. 'Ethnicity Beyond Compare' in *The British Journal of Sociology* 38 (2) (1987), pp. 227–82.

Fleming, R. M. 'Human Hybrids' in *Eugenics Review* 21 (4) (1929–30), pp. 257–63.

Fleming, R. M. and Martin, W. J. *A Study of Growth and Development: Observations in Successive Years on the Same Children* (London: HMSO, 1933).

Fleming, R. M. *Annals of Eugenics* 9 (1939), pp. 55–81.

Fletcher, M. E. *Report on an Investigation into the Colour Problem in Liverpool and other Ports* (Liverpool: Association for the Welfare of Half-Caste Children, 1930).

Fletcher, M. E. 'The Colour Problem in Liverpool' in *Liverpool Review* 5 (1930b), pp. 421–4.

Frankenburg, R. *The Social Construction of Whiteness: White Women, Race Matters* (London: Routledge, 1993).

Fredrickson, G. M. *The Black Image in the White Mind* (New York: Harper & Row, 1971).

Fredrickson, G. M. *White Supremacy: A Comparative Study in American and South African History* (New York: Oxford University Press, 1981).

Frisby, M. K. 'Black, White or Other' in *Emerge* (Dec./Jan. 1996), pp. 48–52.

Frost, D. *The Kru in Freetown and Liverpool: A Study of Maritime work and Community during the 19th and 20th Centuries* (Unpublished Ph.D. thesis: University of Liverpool, 1992).

Frost, D. (1993) 'Ethnic Identity, Transience and Settlement: The Kru in Liverpool Since the Late Nineteenth Century' in *Immigrants and Minorities* 12 (3) (1993), pp. 88–106.

Fryer, P. *Staying Power: The History of Black People in Britain* (London: Pluto, 1984).

Fryer, P. *Black People in the British Empire: An Introduction* (London: Pluto, 1988).

Funeburg, L. *Black, White, Other: Biracial Americans Talk About Race and Identity* (New York: Quill, 1994).

Giddens, A. *Modernity and Self-Identity: Self and Society in the late Modern Age* (Cambridge: Polity, 1991).

Gifford, A. M., Brown, W., Bundey, R. *Loosen the Shackles: First Report of the Liverpool 8 Enquiry into Race Relations in Liverpool* (London: Karia, 1989).

Gill, A. *Ruling Passions: Sex, Race and Empire* (London: BBC Books, 1995).

Gilroy, P. *There Ain't No Black in the Union Jack* (London: Hutchinson, 1987).

Gilroy, P. 'The End of Anti-Racism' in *New Community* 17 (1) (1990), pp. 71–83.

Gilroy, P. *The Black Atlantic: Modernity and Double Consciousness* (London: Verso, 1993).

Gilroy, P. *Small Acts: Thoughts on the Politics of Black Cultures* (London: Serpent's Tail, 1993).

Gilroy, P. 'Roots and Routes: Black Identity as an Outernational Project' in H. W. Harris, H. C. Blue and E. E. H. Griffith (eds), *Racial and Ethnic Identity: Psychological Development and Creative Expression* (New York: Routledge, 1995), pp. 15–30.

Gist, N. P. and Dworkin, A. G. *The Blending of Races: Marginality and Identity in World Perspective* (New York: Wiley-Interscience, 1972).

Goffman, E. *Encounters: Two Studies in the Sociology of Interaction* (Indianapolis: Bobbs-Merrill, 1961).

Goffman, E. *Stigma: Notes on the Management of Spoiled Identity* (Englewood Cliffs, NJ: Prentice-Hall, 1963).

Goldin, I. *Making Race: The Politics and Economics of Coloured Identity in South Africa* (London: Longman, 1987).

Gordon, P. and Klug, F. *New Right New Racism* (Nottingham: Searchlight, 1986).

Granby Toxteth Community Project. *A Survey of the Somali Community in Liverpool: An Indepth Analysis, June 1993* (Liverpool: GTCP, 1993).

Granby Toxteth Community Project. *1991 Census: Key Statistics and Analysis* (Liverpool: GTCP, 1994).

Green, J. 'George William Christian: Liverpool Merchant' in R. Lotz and I. Pegg (eds), *Under the Imperial Carpet: Essays in Black History* (Crawley, UK: Rabbit, 1986).

Griffith, J. H. *Black Like Me* (London: Collins, 1962).

Hall, C. C. I. '2001: A Race Odyssey' in M. P. P. Root (ed.), *The Multiracial Experience: Racial Borders as the New Frontier* (California: Sage, 1996), pp. 395–410.

Hall, S., Critcher, C., Jefferson, T., Clarke, J., Roberts, B. *Policing the Crisis: Mugging, the State and Law and Order* (London: Macmillan, 1978).

Hall, S. 'Racism and Reaction' in *Five Views of Multi-Racial Britain* (London: Commission for Racial Equality, 1978), pp. 23–35.

Hall, S. *Drifting in a Law and Order Society* (London: The Cobden Trust, 1979).

Hall, S. 'Cultural Identity and Diaspora' in J. Rutherford (ed.), *Identity: Community, Culture, Difference* (London: Lawrence & Wishart, 1990), pp. 222–37.

Hall, S. 'New Ethnicities' in J. Donald and A. Rattansi (eds), *'Race', Culture & Difference* (London: Sage & OUP, 1992), pp. 252–9.

Hall, S. 'The West and the Rest' in S. Hall and B. Gieben (eds), *Formations of Modernity* (London: Polity, in association with The Open University, 1992), pp. 275–331.

Hall, S. 'The Question of Cultural Identity' in S. Hall, D. Held, T. McGrew (eds), *Modernity and its Futures* (London: Polity, in association with The Open University, 1992), pp. 273–325.

Hall, S. 'Minimal Selves' in H. A. Baker, M. Diawara, R. H. Lindeborg (eds), *Black British Cultural Studies: A Reader* (Chicago: University of Chicago, 1996), pp. 114–19.

Hamilton, H. J. B. 'Jungle Fever? Jungle Fraud?' in *Interrace Magazine* (Spring/Summer 1993), pp. 20–8.

Harding, V. *There Is A River: The Black Struggle for Freedom in America* (New York: Vintage, 1983; first published 1981).

Harris, H. W., Blue, H. C. and Griffith, E. H. (eds) *Racial and Ethnic Identity: Psychological Development and Creative Expression* (London: Routledge, 1995).

Heineman, B. *The Politics of the Powerless: A Study of the Campaign Against Racial Discrimination* (London: Oxford University for IRR, 1972).

Helmond, M. and Palmer, D. *Staying Power: Black Presence in Liverpool* (UK: NMGM, 1991).

Helms, J. E. (ed.), *Black and White Racial Identity: Theory, Research, and Practice* (London: Praeger, 1993).

Henriques, F. *Family and Colour in Jamaica* (London: Eyre & Spottiswoode, 1953).

Henriques, F. *Children of Caliban: Miscegenation* (London: Secker & Warburg, 1974).

Henriques, F. *Children of Conflict: A Study of Interracial Sex and Marriage* (New York: Dutton, 1975).

Henry, K. S. 'Caribbean Political Dilemmas in North America and in the United Kingdom' in *Journal of Black Studies* 7 (4) (1977), pp. 373–86.

Hesse, B. 'Black to Front and Black Again: Racialization Through Contested Times and Spaces' in Michael Keith and Steve Pile (eds), *Place and the Politics of Identity* (London: Routledge, 1993), pp. 162–82.

Heuman, G. J. *Between Black and White: Race, Politics, and the Free Coloreds in Jamaica, 1792–1865* (Oxford: Clio, 1981).

Hill, C. S. *Immigration and Integration: A Study of the Settlement of Coloured Minorities in Britain* (Oxford: Pergamon, 1970).

Hobsbawm, E. J. *Industry and Empire* (London: Pelican, 1969).

Hoetink, H. '"Race" and Color in the Caribbean' in S. W. Mintz and S. Price (eds), *Caribbean Contours* (Baltimore: Johns Hopkins University Press, 1985).

Holmes, C. (ed.), *Immigrants and Minorities in British Society* (London: George Allen & Unwin, 1978).

Holmes, C. *John Bull's Island: Immigration & British Society, 1871–1971* (London: Macmillan, 1988).

Hoogvelt, A. M. M. 'Ethnocentricism, Authoritarianism and Powellism' in *Race* 21 (1) (1969), pp. 1–12.

hooks, b. *Killing Rage: Ending Racism* (London: Penguin, 1996).

Hooper, R. *Colour in Britain* (London: BBC, 1965).

Hornsby-Smith, M. 'Gaining Access' in Nigel Gilbert (ed.), *Researching Social Life* (London: Sage, 1993), pp. 52–67.

Horton, J. O. *Free People of Colour: Inside the African American Community* (Washington: Smithsonian Institution, 1993).

Hughes, L. 'Mulatto' in *Three Negro Plays* (England: Penguin, 1969; first published in 1935), pp. 19–61.

Humphry, D. *Police Power and Black People* (London: Panther Books, 1972).

Husband, C. (ed.), *Race in Britain: Continuity and Change* (London: Hutchinson, 1982).

Husband, C. *Race and British Society* (Milton Keynes: Open University Press, 1982).

Hyde, F. E. *Liverpool & The Mersey: The Development of a Port 1700–1970* (Bristol: Newton Abbot, 1971).

Ifekwunigwe, J. O. 'Diaspora's Daughters, Africa's Orphans? On Lineage, Authenticity and "Mixed Race" Identity' in H. S. Mirza (ed.), *Black British Feminism: A Reader* (London: Routledge, 1997).

Jackson, P. (ed.), *Race and Racism: Essays in Social Geography* (London: Allen & Unwin, 1987).

Jacobs, J. H. 'Identity Development in Biracial Children' in M. P. P. Root (ed.), *Racially Mixed People in America* (London: Sage, 1992), pp. 190–206.

James, A. '"Black": An Inquiry in the Pejorative Associations of an English Word' in *New Community* 9 (1) (1981), pp. 19–29.

Jenkinson, J. 'Race Riots in Britain' in R. Lotz and I. Pegg (eds), *Under the Imperial Carpet: Essays in Black History 1780–1950* (Crawley, UK: Rabbit, 1986).

Jenkinson, J. *The 1919 Race Riots in Britain: Their Background and Consequences* (Unpublished Ph.D. thesis: Universiy of Edinburgh, 1987).

John, A. *Race in the Inner City* (London: Runneymede Trust, 1972).

Johnson, R. E. *In Words and Pictures: Bill Cosby* (Chicago: Johnson Publishing, 1986).

Jones, G. 'Eugenics and Social Policy Between the Wars' in *Historical Journal* 25 (1982), pp. 717–28.

Jones, R. *The American Connection: The Story of Liverpool's Links with America from Christopher Columbus to The Beatles* (Merseyside: R. Jones, 1992).

Jones, S. *Black Culture, White Youth* (London: Macmillan, 1984).

Jones, S. *The Language of Genes* (London: Flamingo, 1994).

Jones, T. *Britain's Ethnic Minorities: An Analysis of the Labour Force Survey* (London: Policy Studies Institute, 1993).

Jordan, W. *White Over Black: American Attitudes Toward the Negro, 1550–1812* (Baltimore, Md.: Penguin, 1968).

Julienne, L. *Charles Wootton: 1919 Race Riots in Liverpool* (Liverpool: Charles Wootton, 1979).

Karenga, M. *Essays on Struggle: Position and Analysis* (San Diego: Kawaida, 1978).

Karenga, M. *Introduction to Black Studies*, 2nd edn (Los Angeles: University of Sankore, 1993).

Kannan, C. T. *Inter-Racial Marriages in London: A Comparative Study* (London: C. T. Kannan, 1972).

Katz, I. *Stigma: A Social Psychological Analysis* (New Jersey: Lawrence Erlbaum Associates, 1981).

Kaufman, D. 'Mixed Messages: Biracial Experiences in the US' in *Interrace Magazine* (April 1994), pp. 14–19.

Keith, M. 'The 1948 "Race Riots" in Liverpool' in *A Journal of International Migration and Ethnic Relations* 1 (13) (1992), pp. 5–31.

Keith, M. and Pile, S. (eds) *Place and the Politics of Identity* (London: Routledge, 1993).

Kerr, M. *Personality and Conflict in Jamaica* (Liverpool: The University of Liverpool Press, 1952).

Khan, K. and Smith, N. L. *Race, Ethnicity & Culture in the British Context* (London: Avaanca, 1995).

Killingray, D. (ed.), *Africans in Britain* (London: Frank Cass, 1994).

King, C. and King, H. 'The Two Nations': The Life and Work of Liverpool University Settlement and its Associated Institutions, 1906–1937* (London: Hodder & Stoughton and the University of Liverpool Press, 1939).

Klineberg, O. *Characteristics of the American Negro* (New York: Harper and Row, 1944).

Kossoff, J. 'Race and Favour' in *Time Out* (5–12 June 1996), p. 12.

Kuper, L. *Race, Class and Power: Ideology and Revolutionary Change in Pluralist Societies* (London: Duckworth, 1974).

Kuper, L. (ed.), *Race, Science and Society* (Paris: UNESCO Press; New York: Columbia University, 1975).

Kyprianou, P. and Rooney, B. *Third European Anti-Poverty Programme Granby Toxteth: Interim Background Report, Summary Extract* (Liverpool: University of Liverpool, Race and Social Policy Unity, 1991).

Lacey, L. (ed.), *The History of Liverpool from 1207–1907: Some Notes. 700th Anniversary Souvenir* (Liverpool: Liverpool University Press, 1907).

Lane, T. *Liverpool: Gateway of Empire* (London: Lawrence & Wishart, 1987).

Larson, E. J. *Sex, Race and Science: Eugenics in the Deep South* (Baltimore, Md.: John Hopkins University, 1995).

Law, I. and Henfrey, J. *A History of Race and Racism in Liverpool: 1660–1950* (Liverpool: MCRC, 1981).

Law, I. G. *White Racism and Black Settlement in Liverpool: A Study of Local Inequalities and Policies with Particular Reference to Council Housing* (Unpublished Ph.D. thesis, University of Liverpool, 1985).

Lawrence, E. 'Just Plain Commonsense: The "Roots" of Racism' in Centre for Contemporary Cultural Studies (eds), *The Empire Strikes Back: Race and Racism in 1970s Britain* (London: Hutchinson, 1982).

Layton-Henry, Z. and Rich, P. B. (eds) *Race, Government & Politics in Britain* (London: Macmillan, 1986).

Little, K. *Race and Society* (France: UNESCO, 1953).

Little, K. *Negroes in Britain: A Case Study of Racial Relations in English Society* (London: Routledge & Kegan Paul, 1972).

Liverpool Black Caucus. *Racial Politics of Militant in Liverpool: The Black Community's Struggle for Participation in Local Politics 1980–1986* (London: MAPG & Runneymede Trust, 1986).

Liverpool City Council. *The Quality of Life Survey* (Liverpool: LCC, 1991).

Liverpool Youth Organisations Committee. *Special but Not Separate* (Liverpool: Liverpool Council of Social Service, 1968).

Lorimer, D. A. *Color, Caste, and the Victorian English Attitude to the Negro in the Mid-Nineteenth Century* (Leicester: Leicester University, 1978).

Lorimer, D. A. 'Black Slaves and English Liberty: A Re-examination of Racial Slavery in England', *Immigrants and Minorities* 3 (2) (1984), pp. 121–50.

Lotz, R. and Pegg, I. (eds) *Under the Imperial Carpet: Essays in Black History, 1780–1950* (Crawley, UK: Rabbit, 1986).

Lunn, K. (ed.), *Race and Labour in Twentieth Century Britain* (London: Cass, 1985).

Lunn, K. *Hosts, Immigrants, and Minorities: Historical Responses to Newcomers in British Society, 1870–1914* (Folkstone, UK: Davison, 1980).

Lunn, K. and Thurlow, R. C. (eds) *British Facism: Essays on the Radical Right in Inter-War Britain* (London: Croom Helm, 1980).

Macey, M. '"Same Race" Adoption Policy: Anti-Racism or Racism?' in *Journal of Social Policy* 24 (4) (1995), pp. 473–91.

Madan, R. *Coloured Minorities in Great Britain: A Comprehensive Bibliography, 1970–1977* (London: Aldwych, 1979).

Maddox, H. 'The Assimilation of Negroes in a Dockland Area in Britain', *The Sociological Review* (July 1960), pp. 5–15.

Madhubuti, H. R. *Black Men: Obsolete, Single, Dangerous?: Afrikan American Families in Transition: Essays in Discovery, Solution and Hope* (Chicago: Third World Press, 1990).

Mandela, N. *Long Walk to Freedom: The Autobiography of Nelson Mandela* (London: Little, Brown, 1994).

Manley, D. R. *The Social Structure of the Liverpool Negro Community, with Special Reference to the Formation of Formal Associations* (Unpublished Ph.D. thesis: University of Liverpool, 1959).

Manning, M. 'On the Tebbit Express' in *New Statesman & Society* (9 Dec. 1989).

Marke, E. *In Troubled Waters: Memoirs of Seventy Years in England* (London: Karia, 1986; originally published under the title: *Old Man Trouble*, 1975).

Maxime, J. E. 'Some Psychological Models of Black Self-Concept' in S. Ahmed, J. Cheetam, and J. Small (eds), *Social Work with Black Children and their Families* (London: Batsford, 1986), pp. 100–16.

Maxime, J. E. *Black Like Me, Work Book Three: Mixed Parentage* (London: Emani, 1994).

May, R. and Cohen, R. 'The Interaction Between Race and Colonialism: A Case Study of the Liverpool Race Riots of 1919' in *Race and Class* 16 (2) (1974), pp. 111–26.

Mayfield, K. 'Mixed Emotions' in *Interrace Magazine* 6 (6) (1995), pp. 22–5.

McCullough, J. *Black Soul, White Artifact: Fanon's Clinical Psychology and Social Theory* (Cambridge: Cambridge University Press, 1983).

MCRC, LBC, MAPG. *Racial Discrimination and Disadvantage in Employment in Liverpool: Evidence Submitted to the House of Commons Select Committee on Employment* (Liverpool: MAPG, 1986).

Members of Merseyside Socialist Research Group. *Genuinely Seeking Work: Mass Unemployment on Merseyside in the 1930s* (Merseyside, UK: Liver Press, 1992).

Memmi, A. *The Colonizer and the Colonized* (London: Earthscan, 1990; first published in 1965).

Merseyside Area Manpower Board. *Ethnic Minorities in Liverpool: Problems Faced in their Search for Work* (Merseyside: Manpower Services Commission, 1985).

Merseyside Area Profile Group. *Racial Disadvantage in Liverpool: An Area Profile* (Liverpool: MAPG, 1980).

Merseyside Information Service. *Granby Toxteth Skills Audit* (Liverpool: MIS, 1994).

Miles, R. *Racism & Migrant Labour* (London: Routledge & Kegan Paul, 1982).

Miles, R. 'The Riots of 1958: Notes on the Ideological Construction of "Race Relations" as a Political Issue in Britain' in *Immigrants and Minorities* 3 (3) (1984), pp. 252–7.

Miles, R. 'Marxism Versus the Sociology of "Race Relations"?' in *Ethnic and Racial Studies* 7 (2) (1984), pp. 217–37.

Miles, R. and Phizacklea, A. *White Man's Country: Racism in British Politics* (London: Pluto, 1984).

Miles, R. 'Racism, Ideology and Disadvantage' in *Social Studies Review* 5 (4) (1990), pp. 148–51.

Mills, C. Wright. *The Sociological Imagination* (London: Oxford University Press, 1959).

Mills, C. W. *The Racial Contract* (Ithaca: Cornell University Press, 1997).

Milner, D. *Children and Race* (Harmondsworth: Penguin, 1975).

Milner, D. *Children and Race Ten Years On* (London: Ward Lock Educational, 1983).

Modood, T., Beishon, S. and Virdee, S. *Changing Ethnic Identities* (London: Policy Studies Institute, 1994).

Modood, T. and Berthoud, R. et al. *Ethnic Minorities in Britain: Diversity and Disadvantage* (London: Policy Studies Institute, 1997).

Montagu, A. *Statement on Race: An Annotated Elaboration and Exposition of the Four Statements on Race Issued by The United Nations Educational, Scientific, and Cultural Organization* (London: Oxford University Press, 1972).

Moore, R. *Racism and Black Resistance in Britain* (London: Pluto, 1975).

Moore, R. *Ethnic Statistics and the 1991 Census – the Black Population of Inner Liverpool* (London: Runneymede, 1994).

Morris, S. 'Moody: The Forgotten Visionary' in *New Community* 1 (3) (1972), pp. 193–6.

Morrison, T. *The Bluest Eye* (London: Picador, 1990).

Muir, R. *History of Liverpool* (London: Williams & Norgate, 1907).

Muir, R. *A Short History of the British Commonwealth*, vol. 1, 2nd edn (London: George Philip & Son, 1922).

Mullard, C. *Race, Class and Ideology: Some Formal Notes* (London: University of London, 1985).

Murari, T. *The New Savages* (London: Macmillan, 1975).

Murphy, A. *From the Empire to the Rialto: Racism and Reaction in Liverpool 1918–1948* (Merseyside: Liver Press, 1995).

Myers, L. J. *Understanding an Afrocentric World View: Introduction to Optimal Psychology*, 2nd edn (Iowa: Kendal/Hunt, 1988).

Myrdal, G. *An American Dilemma*, vols 1 & 2 (New York: Harper & Row, 1944).

Nash, P. T. 'Multicultural Identity and the Death of Stereotypes' in M. P. P. Root (ed.), *Racially Mixed People in America* (London: Sage, 1992).

New Society. 'Anatomy of a Riot' (17 Aug. 1972), pp. 336–7.

Nobles, W. *Standing in the River: African (Black) Psychology: Transformed and Transforming* (London: Karia, 1992).

O'Mara, P. *The Autobiography of a Liverpool Irish Slummy* (London: Hopkinson, 1934).

Park, R. E. 'Human Migration and the Marginal Man' in *The American Journal of Sociology* 33 (6) (1928), pp. 881–93.

Park, R. E. 'Mentality of Racial Hybrids' in *The American Journal of Sociology* 36 (1930), pp. 535–51.

Park, R. E. *Race and Culture*, vol. 1 (Glencoe, Ill.: The Free Press, 1950).

Parmar, P. 'Black Feminism: The Politics of Articulation', in J. Rutherford (ed.), *Identity: Community, Culture, Difference* (London: Lawrence & Wishart, 1990), pp. 101–26.

Patterson, O. *Slavery and Social Death: A Comparative Study* (London: Harvard University Press, 1982).

Patterson, S. *Colour and Culture in South Africa: A Study of the Status of the Cape Coloured People within the Social Structure of South Africa* (London: Routledge & Kegan Paul, 1953).

Patterson, S. *Dark Strangers: A Sociological Study of a Recent West Indian Migrant Group in Brixton, South London* (London: Penguin, 1963).

Peach, C. *West Indian Migration to Britain: A Social Geography* (London: Oxford Universiy Press, 1968).

Peach, C., Robinson, V. and Smith, S. *Ethnic Segregation in Cities* (London: Croom Helm, 1981).

Pearson, D. G. *Race, Class and Political Activism: A Study of West Indians in Britain* (Farnborough: Gower, 1981).

Pinderhughes, E. 'Biracial Identity – Asset or Handicap?', in H. W. Harris, H. C. Blue, and E. E. H. Griffith (eds), *Racial and Ethnic Identity: Psychological Development and Creative Expression* (New York: Routledge, 1995), pp. 73–93.

Poliakov, L. *The Aryan Myth* (London: Chatto, 1974).

Political and Economic Planning. *Colonial Students in Britain: A Report* (London: PEP, 1955).

Priestley, J. B. *English Journey: Being A Rambling But Truthful Account Of What One Man Saw And Heard And Felt And Thought During A Journey Through England During the Autumn Of The Year 1933* (London: Penguin, 1977; first published in 1934).

Pryce, K. *Endless Pressure* (Harmondsworth: Penguin, 1979).

Rack, P. *Race, Culture and Mental Disorder* (London: Tavistock, 1982).

Ramdin, R. *The Making of the Black Working Class in Britain* (Aldershot, UK: Gower, 1987).

Ramirez, D. A. 'Multiracial Identity in a Color-Conscious World' in M. M. P. Root (ed.), *The Multiracial Experience: Racial Borders as the New Frontier* (London: Sage, 1996), pp. 49–62.

Rex, J. *Race Relations in Sociological Theory* (London: Weidenfeld and Nicolson, 1970).

Rex, J. and Tomlinson, S. *Colonial Immigrants in a British City: A Class Analysis* (London: Routledge and Kegan Paul, 1979).

Rex, J. 'A Working Paradigm for Race Relations Research' in *Ethnic and Racial Studies* 4 (1) (1981), pp. 1–25.

Reynolds, V. 'Biology and Race Relations' in *Ethnic and Racial Studies* 6 (2–3) (1986), pp. 209–21.

Rich, P. B. 'Philanthropic Racism in Britain: The Liverpool University Settlement, the Anti-Slavery Society and the Issue of "Half-Caste" Children, 1919–51' in *Immigrants and Minorities* 3 (1) (1984), pp. 69–88.

Rich, P. B. and Layton-Henry, Z. (eds) *Race, Government and Politics in Britain* (London: Macmillan, 1986).

Rich, P. B. 'Conservative Ideology and Race in Modern British Politics' in Z. Layton-Henry and P. B. Rich (eds), *Race, Government and Politics in Britain* (London: Macmillan, 1986), pp. 45–72.

Rich, P. B. *Race and Empire in British Politics* (Cambridge: Cambridge University, 1986).

Rich, P. B. 'The Black Diaspora in Britain: Afro-Caribbean Students and the Struggle for a Political Identity, 1900–1950' in *Immigrants and Minorities* 6 (2) (1987), pp. 151–73.

Rich, P. B. 'The Politics of "Race Relations" in Britain and the West' in P. Jackson (ed.), *Race and Racism: Essays in Social Geography* (London: Allen & Unwin, 1987), pp. 95–118.

Rich, P. B. *Essays on Race, Culture and English Society: Prospero's Return* (London: Hansib, 1994).

Richards, W. 'Working with "Mixed Race" Young People' in *Youth Policy* (49) (Summer 1995), pp. 62–72.

Richmond, A. H. 'Economic Insecurity and Stereotypes as Factors in Colour Prejudice' in *The Sociological Review* 42 (8) (1950), pp. 147–70.

Richmond, A. H. *Assimilation and Adjustment of a Group of West Indian Negroes in England: A Case of Inter-Group Relations* (Unpublished MA thesis: University of Liverpool, 1951).

Richmond, A. H. *Colour Prejudice in Britain: A Study of West Indian Workers in Liverpool, 1941–1951* (London: Routledge & Kegan Paul, 1954).

Richmond, A. H. *The Colour Problem: A Study of Race Relations* (Harmondsworth: Penquin, 1955).

Richmond, A. H. (ed.), *Readings in Race and Ethnic Relations* (Oxford: Pergamon, 1972).

Roberts, Y. 'Boys with the Greenbacks' in *New Statesman & Society* (9 Dec. 1988).

Rodney, W. *The Groundings with My Brothers* (London: Bogle-L'Overture, 1975).

Rogers, J. A. *Sex and Race: A Study of White, Negro, and Indian Miscegenation in the Two Americas* (3 vols) (USA: Helga M. Rogers, 1940–4).

Rogers, J. *Young Black People in Liverpool 8* (Unpublished report, 1975).

Root, M. P. P. (ed.), *Racially Mixed People in America* (London: Sage, 1992).

Root, M. P. P. (ed.), *The Multiracial Experience: Racial Borders as the New Frontier* (London: Sage, 1996).

Rose, E. J. B. et al. *Colour and Citizenship* (London: IRR, 1969).

Ross, L. 'Mixed Blessing' in *Pride* (Feb./March 1995), pp. 40–2.

Russell, K., Wilson, M. and Hall, R. *The Color Complex: The Politics of Skin Color Among African Americans* (New York: Harcourt Brace Jovanovich, 1992).

Rutherford, J. (ed.), *Identity: Community, Culture, Difference* (London: Lawrence & Wishart, 1990).

Said, E. W. *Orientalism* (London: Penguin, 1987; first published in 1978).

Scarman, L. *The Brixton Disorders, 10–12 April 1981*, Cmnd 8427 (London: HMSO, 1981).

Schiele, J. H. 'Organizational Theory from An Afrocentric Perspective' in *Journal of Black Studies* 21 (2) (1990), pp. 145–61.

Scobie, E. *Black Britannia: A History of Blacks in Britain* (Chicago: Johnson Publishing, 1972).

Seabrook, J. 'Land of Broken Toys' in *New Statesman & Society* (11 Sept. 1992).

Searle, G. R. *Eugenics and Politics in Britain: 1900–1914* (Leyden: Noordhoff International, 1976).

Searle-Chatterjee, M. 'Colour Symbolism and the Skin: Some Notes' in *New Community* 9 (1) (1981), pp. 31–5.

Segal, R. *The Race War: The World-Wide Conflict of Races* (Harmondsworth: Penguin, 1967).

Segal, R. *The Black Diaspora* (London: Faber and Faber, 1995).

Shaefer, R. T. 'Intermarriage in Britain and the United States' in *Patterns of Prejudice* 15 (2) (1981), pp. 8–15.

Shapiro, H. L. 'Race Mixture' in UNESCO (eds), *Race and Science* (New York: Columbia University Press, 1969), pp. 343–89.

Sherwood, M. *Many Struggles: West Indian Workers and Service Personnel in Britain (1939–1945)* (London: Karia, 1984).

Sherwood, M. *Pastor Daniels Ekarte and the African Churches Mission* (London: The Savannah Press, 1994).

Shipman, P. *The Evolution of Racism: Human Differences and the Use and Abuse of Science* (New York: Simon & Schuster, 1994).

Simey, T. S. *Welfare and Planning in the West Indies* (London: Oxford University Press, 1946).

Sivanandan, A. *Coloured Minorities in Britain: A Select Bibliography*, 3rd edn (London: IRR, 1969).

Sivanandan, A. *Race and Resistance: The IRR Story* (London: Race Today, 1974).

Sivanandan, A. *A Different Hunger: Writings on Black Resistance* (London: Pluto, 1982).

Sivanandan, A. *From Resistance to Rebellion: Asian and Afro-Caribbean Struggles in Britain* (London: IRR, 1986).

Sivanandan, A. 'Race Against Time' in *New Statesman & Society* (15 Oct. 1993), pp. 16–17.

Sivanandan, A. *Communities of Resistance: Writings on Black Struggles for Socialism* (London: Verso, 1990).

Skellington, R. and Morris, P. *Race in Britain Today* (London: Sage, 1992).

Skidmore, T. E. *Black into White: Race and Nationality in Brazilian Thought* (Durham, NC and London: Duke University Press, 1993).

Small, J. 'Transracial Placements: Conflicts and Contradictions' in S. Ahmed, J. Cheetham, and J. Small (eds), *Social Work with Black Children and their Families* (London: Batsford, 1986), pp. 81–99.

Small, S. 'Attaining Racial Parity in the United States and England: We Got to Go Where the Greener Grass Grows', *Sage Race Relations Abstracts* 16 (3) (1991), pp. 3–55.

Small, S. 'Racialised Relations in Liverpool: A Contemporary Anomaly' in *New Community* 17 (4) (1991), pp. 511–537.

Small, S. 'Half-breed is a Scurrilous Demeaning and Degrading Term' in *Caribbean Times* (14 July 1992).

Small, S. *Racialised Barriers: The Black Experience in the United States and England in the 1980s* (London: Routledge, 1994).

Smith, L. T. *Decolonizing Methodologies: Research and Indigenous Peoples* (London: Zed Books, 1999).

Snowdon, F. M., Jr. *Before Colour Prejudice: The Ancient View of Blacks* (Cambridge: Harvard University Press, 1983).

Snyder, L. L. *The Idea of Racialism: Its Meaning and History* (Princeton, NJ: Van Nostrand, 1962).

Solomos, J. *Black Youth, Racism and the State: The Politics of Ideology and Policy* (Cambridge: Cambridge University Press, 1988).

Solomos, J. *Race and Racism in Contemporary Britain* (Basingstoke: Macmillan, 1989).

Solomos, J. 'Changing Forms of Racial Discourse' in *Social Studies Review* 6 (2) (1990), pp. 74–8.

Spencer, J. M. *The New Colored People: The Mixed-Race Movement in America* (New York: New York University Press, 1997).

Spencer, R. 'The "M" Word' in *Interrace Magazine* (March 1994), p. 29.

Spencer-Strachan, L. *Confronting the Color Crisis in the Afrikan Diaspora: Emphasis Jamaica* (New York: African World Infosystems, 1992).

Spickard, P. *Mixed Blood: Intermarriage and Ethnic Identity in Twentieth-Century America* (Madison: University of Wisconsin Press, 1989).

Spickard, P. R. 'The Illogic of American Racial Categories' in M. P. P. Root (ed.), *Racially Mixed People in America* (London: Sage, 1992), pp. 12–23.

Stack, C. B. *All Our Kin: Strategies for Survival in a Black Community* (New York: Harper & Row, 1975).

Staples, R. *Introduction to Black Sociology* (New York: McGraw-Hill, 1976).

Stepan, N. *The Idea of Race in Science: Great Britain 1800–1960* (London: Macmillan, 1982).

Stephan, C. W. 'Mixed-Heritage Individuals: Ethnic Identity and Trait Characteristics' in M. P. P. Root (ed.), *Racially Mixed People in America* (London: Sage, 1992).

Stonequist, E. V. *Marginal Man: A Study of Personality and Culture Conflict* (New York: Russell & Russell, 1961; 1937).

Thompson, D. C. *Sociology of the Black Experience* (Wesport, Conn.: Greenwood, 1974).

Thorton, M. C. 'Is Multiracial Status Unique? The Personal and Social Experience' in M. P. P. Root (ed.), *Racially Mixed People in America* (London: Sage, 1992), pp. 321–5.

Thorton, M. C. 'Hidden Agendas, Identity Theories, and Multiracial People' in M. P. P. Root (ed.), *The Multiracial Experience: Racial Borders as the New Frontier* (London: Sage, 1996), pp. 101–20.

Tibbles, A. (ed.) *Transatlantic Slavery: Against Human Dignity* (London: HMSO for National Museums & Galleries on Merseyside, 1994).

Tizard, B. and Phonenix, A. *Black, White or Mixed Race?: Race and Racism in the Lives of Young People Mixed Parentage* (London: Routledge, 1993).

Torkington, N. P. K. *The Racial Politics of Health: A Liverpool Profile* (Liverpool: MAPG, 1983).

Torkington, N. P. K. *Racism in the National Health Service: A Liverpool Profile* (Unpublished Ph.D. thesis: University of Liverpool, 1985).

Torkington, N. P. K. *Black Health: A Political Issue* (Glasgow: CARJ & LIHE, 1991).

Trollope, A. *The West Indies and the Spanish Main* (New York: Hippocrene, 1985; first published in 1859).

Twine, F. W. 'Heterosexual Alliances: The Romantic Management of Racial Identity' in M. P. P. Root (ed.), *The Multiracial Experience: Racial Borders as the New Frontier* (London: Sage, 1996), pp. 291–304.

UNESCO. *Race and Science* (New York: Columbia University Press, 1951).

UNESCO. 'Proposals on the Aspects of Race', Aug. 1964, Moscow Statement on 'Race' published in *Race* 6 (1965), pp. 243–7.

UNESCO *4th Statement on Race and Racial Prejudice* (Paris: UNESCO, 1967).

Van den Berghe, P. L. *Race and Racism: A Comparative Perspective*, 2nd edn (New York: John Wiley, 1978; first published in 1967).

Venner, M. 'What the Papers Said About Scarman' in *New Community* 9 (3) (1982), pp. 354–63.

Waller, P. J. *Democracy and Sectarianism: A Political and Social History of Liverpool, 1868–1939* (Liverpool: University of Liverpool, 1981).

Waller, P. J. 'The Riots in Toxteth, Liverpool; A Survey' in *New Community* 9 (3) (1982), pp. 344–53.

Walvin, J. *Black and White: The Negro and English Society, 1555–1945* (London: Allen Lane, 1973).

Walvin, J. *Black Ivory: A History of British Slavery* (London: Fontana, 1993).

Washington, D. 'On Being Biracial' in *Interrace Magazine* (June/July 1994), pp. 27–8.

Watson, J. L. (ed.), *Between Two Cultures: Migrants and Minorities in Britain* (Oxford: Blackwell, 1977).

Watts, C. *Black Prospects: A Report on the Job Prospects of Liverpool-born Blacks* (Liverpool: South Liverpool Personnel, 1978).

Weber, M. *The Theory of Economic and Social Organisation* (Glencoe, Ill.: The Free Press, 1947).

Weisman, J. R. 'An "Other" Way of Life: The Empowerment of Alterity in the Interracial Individual' in M. P. P. Root (ed.), *The Multiracial Experience: Racial Borders as the New Frontier* (London: Sage, 1996), pp. 152–64.

Whittington-Egan, R. *Liverpool Colonnade* (Liverpool: Philip, Son & Nephew, 1955), pp. 212–15.

Williams, G. *The Liverpool Privateers and the Liverpool Slave Trade* (London: Heinemann, 1897).

Williams, E. *Capitalism and Slavery* (London: Andre Deustch, 1991; first published in 1944).

Williams, T. K. 'Race as Process: Reassessing the "What Are You?" Encounters of Biracial Individuals' in M. P. P. Root (ed.), *The Multiracial Experience: Racial Borders as the New Frontier* (London: Sage, 1996), pp. 191–210.

Williamson, J. *New People: Miscegenation and Mulattoes in the United States* (New York: Free Press, 1980).

Williamson, J. *A Rage for Order: Black/White Relations in the American South Since Emancipation* (New York: Oxford University Press, 1986).

Wilson, A. 'Mixed Race Children: An Exploratory Study of Racial Categorisation and Identity' *New Community* 9 (1) (1981), pp. 36–43.

Wilson, A. *Mixed Race Children: A Study of Identity* (London: Allen & Unwin, 1987).

Wilson, A. N. *The Falsification of Afrikan Consciousness: Eurocentric History, Psychiatry and the Politics of White Supremacy* (New York: African World InfoSystems, 1993).

Wilson, C. E. 'Racism and Private Assistance: The Support of West Indian and African Missions in Liverpool, England, during the Interwar Years' in *African Studies Review* 35 (2) (1992), pp. 55–76.

Wilson, D. *Prehistoric Man: Researches into the Origins of Civilization in the Old and New World*, vol. 2 (Cambridge: Macmillan, 1862).

Winters, C. A. 'Afrocentricism – A Valid Frame of Reference' in *Journal of Black Studies* 25 (2) (1994), pp. 170–90.

Wirth, L. and Goldhamer, H. 'The Hybrid and the Problem of Miscegenation' in O. Klineberg (ed.), *Characteristics of the American Negro* (New York: Harper & Row), part V.

Wolf, E. R. 'Perilous Ideas: Race, Culture, People' in *Current Anthropology* 35 (1) (1994), pp. 1–12.

Woodson, C. G. *The Mis-Education of the Negro* (Trenton, NJ: African World Press, 1990; first published in 1933).

Yeboah, S. K. *The Ideology of Racism* (London: Hansib, 1988).

Young, M. 'On the Mersey Beat' in *The Listerner* (2 Nov. 1978).

Young, R. J. C. *Colonial Desire: Hybridity in Theory, Culture and Race* (London: Routledge, 1995).

Younge, G. 'Row Over Plan for Census Race Labels', *Guardian* (9 Dec. 1996).

Zephaniah, B. *Inna Liverpool* (Stirling, Scotland: AK Press, 1992).

Index